D0091597

"Once again, Myers hits a home ru[...] and with highly informed common [...] us all—church and congregants alike—to honesty about our goals and then offers us sophisticated, efficacious, and grace-filled ways to realize them."

—Phyllis Tickle, contributing editor in religion, *Publishers Weekly*

"Most people think 'deep' and 'practical' can't go together, as if being practical meant being shallow. Joe Myers brings the two together as well as anyone I've ever read. Looking back on twenty-four years of church planting and pastoral ministry, I wish I had thoroughly digested *Organic Community* before I got started. It would have saved so much wasted energy—mine, and those whose lives I foolishly tried to 'master plan.' Beneath its simplicity and practicality lie real depth, and from its depth will flow creative, practical action that will make a difference for years to come. This is a book I will reread and widely recommend."

—Brian McLaren, author/activist; brianmclaren.net

"Helen of Troy may have had the face that launched a thousand ships, but Joe Myers has the furnishings of thought and design that will launch a thousand books, blogs, and briefs on growing 'organic community.' If a classic is something that has never finished what it has to say, then this little gem is a 'classic.'"

—Leonard Sweet, E. Stanley Jones Professor of Evangelism, Drew Theological School; distinguished visiting professor, George Fox University; www.wikiletics.com

"Anyone seeking to mobilize people to collective and cooperative effort or to promote organizational growth will find Joseph Myers's *Organic Community* an invaluable resource. Whether educated about organizational systems or merely experiencing them in schools, sports, the military, work settings, or voluntary associations, we have all gotten used to and accepted many wrongheaded assumptions that run contrary to the organization's goals.

"Myers acknowledges that his is a different kind of how-to book. As much, or more, it is a how-not-to book that exposes fallacies inherent in common organizational policies and procedures, which are all the more destructive in organizations relying on volunteer efforts.

"Myers offers nine tools, not 'steps,' the more of which one masters the more results are achieved. Application of even a few of these tools promises substantial improvement.

"The book comes out of a small groups perspective and is aimed primarily at churches, but the principles set forth have application in organizations of all kinds."

—Ray Oldenburg, emeritus professor of sociology, The University of West Florida; author, *The Great Good Place*

"*Organic Community* is packed with practical wisdom and experience about creating church communities. At a time when many pastors and church leaders flock to the latest models and methods for church growth, Joe Myers asks us to abandon master plans and new programs and, instead, concentrate on shaping social environments where people can thrive and grow and genuinely participate and where community can emerge naturally. This book isn't a manual for church growth; it's more of an invitation to an adventure—with masses of useful advice and guidance for those who take up the challenge. I'd make it required reading for all church leaders."

—Dave Tomlinson, vicar, St. Luke's Church, West Holloway, in North London; author, *The Post-Evangelical* and *Still Waters and Skyscrapers*

"Joe has captured the essence of what it means for the church to be primarily an organism rather than an organization. She is in flux, constantly moving and growing beyond the limitations of the blueprints of a stale, innate object. This book is a 'must read' for preachers and church leaders whose overwhelming desire is to *grow* a church in the way God desires."

—James D. Harless, senior minister, Tri-County Christian Church

"Joe Myers once again challenges people serving through the church to rethink the way people enter community. While providing nine practical tools for assisting people to enter community, there is no linear or formulaic structure, no promise of a 'this is the silver bullet' for ministry. *Organic Community* lives up to its name as it forces readers to reconsider master plan strategy, which rarely worked anyway, in favor of organic order as a means for people seeking community. The nine tools will cause cognitive dissonance for many folks who formerly accepted master plan tools for helping people find community. Such dissonance is valuable even if you don't agree with the tools or the foundation from which Myers constructs organic order. We here at Southland Christian Church are finding many of the concepts Myers uses helpful in our own journey to community. This book will become a 'must read' for our people, as is *The Search to Belong*."

—Myron D. Williams, study minister, Southland Christian Church

"Here is a refreshing look not only at church but also other human institutions in which people connect. It represents a move away from hierarchical and mechanistic institutions in which people are pigeon-holed, to a more relational and organic model in which people can realize their full creative potential within a network of supportive relationships. This approach is especially significant for the church, because institutional models are cumbersome and expensive to reproduce. Organic models of faith—communities, on the other hand—are reproducible and allow for exponential growth. We need many more fresh expressions of church to reach future generations for Christ."

—Eddie Gibbs, Fuller Theological Seminary

**Emergent Village resources for communities of faith**

*An Emergent Manifesto of Hope*
edited by Doug Pagitt and Tony Jones

*Organic Community*
Joseph R. Myers

*Signs of Emergence*
Kester Brewin (July 2007)

*Justice in the Burbs*
Will and Lisa Samson (August 2007)

*Intuitive Leadership*
Tim Keel (October 2007)

**www.emersionbooks.com**

# ORGANIC COMMUNITY

creating
a place
where people
naturally
connect

## joseph r. myers

BakerBooks

Grand Rapids, Michigan

© 2007 by Joseph R. Myers

Published by Baker Books
a division of Baker Publishing Group
P.O. Box 6287, Grand Rapids, MI 49516-6287
www.bakerbooks.com

Third printing, August 2008

Printed in the United States of America

Library of Congress Cataloging-in-Publication Data
Myers, Joseph R., 1962–
    Organic community : creating a place where people naturally con-
nect / Joseph R. Myers.
        p.    cm.
    Includes bibliographical references and index.
    ISBN 10: 0-8010-6598-4 (pbk.)
    ISBN 978-0-8010-6598-9 (pbk.)
        1. Communities—Religious aspects—Christianity.  2. Fellowship—
Religious aspects—Christianity.  3. Pastoral theology.  I. Title
BV4517.5.M93 2007
253—dc22                                            2007000676

Unless otherwise indicated, Scripture is taken from the Holman Christian Standard Bible, copyright 1999, 2000, 2002, 2003 by Holman Bible Publishers. Used by permission.

Scripture marked NIV is taken from the HOLY BIBLE, NEW INTERNATIONAL VERSION®. NIV®. Copyright © 1973, 1978, 1984 by International Bible Society. Used by permission of Zondervan. All rights reserved.

Photographic images provided by www.photospin.com, © Copyright, PhotoSpin, Inc., 2007, all rights reserved.

Author photo by Michael Wilson.

Some of the anecdotal illustrations in this book are true and are included with the permission of the person involved. All other illustrations are composites of true situations, and any resemblance to people living or dead is coincidental.

To my muse:
Who sings to me with her eyes
Hugs me warmly with her smile
And keeps me alive with her love.

ēmersion is a partnership between Baker Books and Emergent Village, a growing, generative friendship among missional Christians seeking to love our world in the Spirit of Jesus Christ. The ēmersion line is intended for professional and lay leaders like you who are meeting the challenges of a changing culture with vision and hope for the future. These books will encourage you and your community to live into God's kingdom here and now.

*Organic Community* is a crucial book in this effort because the importance of pursuing new ways for people to connect and create commonality cannot be overstated. Joe Myers's ability to combine thoughtful insight with practical implications will be welcome among readers from a variety of different settings.

We live in a time when what is needed is not a simple rearranging of options or priorities but rather a clarion call to new frontiers of engagement, interaction, and practices that lead to transformative community. This is what makes *Organic Community* such a vital contribution not only to the ēmersion line but to the lives and thinking of Christians everywhere.

Emergent Village resources for communities of faith

# CONTENTS

# FOREWORD

## by Randy Frazee

He that will not apply new remedies must expect new evils." Francis Bacon, a seventeenth-century philosopher, penned these prophetic words. Accepting a new reality and moving people toward it is the clarion call of leadership. But change and transition can be a difficult task. Machiavelli said, "There is nothing more perilous than change." Because change is so difficult, we often delay moving in the new direction due to the mistaken notion that while things may not get better, they certainly won't get any worse. Now, instead of making the necessary changes, we also must deal with the negative effects of postponing that change.

Twenty-first-century entrepreneur and Emergent Village resident Joe Myers has restated Bacon's prophecy in his own words in this book. While the concepts will have a broad appeal to many leaders from many disciplines, Joe put his crosshairs on the formation of community. This pleases me greatly. A new reality is upon us, and change is already delinquent. For many readers the main idea of Joe's book will be a brand new message. Brace yourself. For the rest of us, we knew it was here but were either afraid to face it or clueless on how to think about it, let alone what to do about it.

What is the main idea? It is a major shift "from programming community to using principles of organic order to develop an environment where community can emerge." In the pit of the stomachs of most church leaders I know, there is this gnawing sense that Christian community has to be more natural, spontaneous, and life-giving. Yet most of us in ministry today have been trained to offer up models that are often overprogrammed and contrived.

Readers beware. Joe is not offering "Organic Community Kits." That is not his style. Rather, he provides a solid framework and makes us think for ourselves. He even encourages us to challenge his thinking. After years of being friends with him, I know that Joe is less interested in people thinking he is right than in good, healthy, honest dialogue taking place on the real issues of community.

Let me tell you how I read this book, because I think it may be a good recommendation for you. Joe presents nine essential tools that capture the fundamental shift to organic community. As you read about each tool, first apply it to your own personal experience. Then, if you are responsible for creating community within your church or small group, honestly assess where your community is in view of these nine principles. Doing this myself has intensified my convictions, sharpened my focus, and given me some new remedies to apply.

Randy Frazee
teaching pastor, Willow Creek Community Church;
author, *The Connecting Church* and *Making Room for Life*

# FOREWORD

## by Bill Donahue

ll learning is the result of failed expectations," a teacher once said. When I heard that statement I began chewing on it, debating it, wrestling with its veracity, and reflecting upon my personal experience. It was provocative, forcing me to think deeply about learning and confronting my illusions about personal change and growth.

In *Organic Community* Joe Myers achieves a similar result—provoking and confronting the reader. Believe me, those are good things. To *provoke* means "to call forth," and to *confront* implies "to turn one's face toward." Joe's writing called me forth—to response, dialogue, debate, evaluation, and thoughtfulness—and challenged me to face my assumptions about planning, power, and leadership. This is why I enjoyed the book and value Joe's friendship so very much.

Here you will be exposed to new language about organizations and new ways of thinking about how individuals and groups connect and thrive. Terms like "responsible anarchy" and "revolving power" will make you assess how you guide and develop people. The assertion that "story is the measure of community . . . the universal measurement of life" will make you ask, "Really? Do I agree?" Joe will invite you to envision the Trinity as a "dance of three verbs," and push you to consider becoming an "environmentalist" instead of a master planner with a grand design for a predictable future. Will such ideas unnerve you? I sure hope so.

Interestingly, my friendship with Joe has often prompted his critics to wonder, "Bill, why do you invite Joe Myers to speak at your small groups conferences? The guy hates small groups, doesn't he?" I can assure you that Joe does not hate any such groups. What drives him crazy, however, are formulaic and programmatic models of communal life that reek of control and manipulation, thrive on the abuse of power, and promote a one-size-fits-all approach to spiritual growth.

In reality, Joe and I agree on a number of issues, and he has influenced my thinking and increased my resolve to recover biblical expressions of communal life in the church. We agree that groups of various kinds have great value for churches, that community cannot be forced upon anyone, and that structures should serve people (not people serve structures). We believe that most individuals are seeking vital relationships with others in a grand mission, not looking to fill slots on someone's prefabricated org chart. The invitation to "Come join us in the great adventure" trumps "Help us achieve our strategy" for both of us. And that is why *Organic Community* is such an important work.

This is an engaging read that will likely leave you disturbed by Joe's assertions, refreshed by his ideas, challenged by his philosophy, and intrigued by his observations—before you even finish the first chapter! So don't read it before bed, unless insomnia is your plan for the evening. I have chewed through it twice. And I know I'll be back to gnaw on it again, because parts of it are still eating at me.

Bill Donahue
executive director of small group, Willow Creek Association;
author, *Leading Life-Changing Small Groups*,
coauthor, *Building a Church of Small Groups*

# AUTHOR'S NOTE

This book is filled with insights gathered from research, interviews, anecdotal observation, and a lab called settingPace. My wife, Sara, and I started settingPace in 1991. Begun as a part-time business, it has evolved into a vibrant community, constantly changing to meet the demands of our clients and marketplace. Together with our partner Minta Berry and our staff, we've had the opportunity to live out these concepts on a daily basis.

Most of these insights are shared through story. Every story is true. And if a story sounds like it is your story, it probably is—yours and a thousand others'. I have changed names and often chosen to merge several stories into one. This makes each story everyone's story, but no one individual's story.

Many have influenced these discoveries. I can't take sole credit. I'm also aware that I'm writing in the midst of a journey of learning. There are many more discoveries to be made, some that will contradict those I have expressed in these pages. So don't hesitate to disagree, argue, and rethink the ideas in this book. I know I will keep doing so as the journey continues.

Contact me and let me know what you find along the way as we continue to learn how healthy communities emerge.

Joe Myers
jmyers@languageofbelonging.com

# INTRODUCTION

## okay, but how?

**A** how-to manual? Depends on how you look at it. During the past several years of traveling, speaking, and returning email related to my book *The Search to Belong*, I received many questions that centered on *how*.

> "*How* do you create a place where people naturally connect?"
>
> "*How* do you stop the tyranny of programs and meetings and become an 'environmentalist'?"
>
> "*How* can I plan and depend on spontaneity and synchronicity?"
>
> "*How* can I make the switch and still keep my job?"

This book is a response to those questions.

In a way, this is a how-to book. But not one with step-by-step instructions. These pages do not contain a secret master plan only now revealed. Herein is no promise of grand success. This

> *Transformation comes more from pursuing profound questions than seek-ing practical answers.*
>
> —Peter Block, *The Answer to How Is Yes*[1]

is a different kind of how-to book. This is a book that discusses a transition of thought.

For me, that transition of thought became real in 1991, as my wife and I started our own company, settingPace. We had been in church ministry and seen how churches adapted business models to grow congregations. "Successful" business practices were brought into the church environment with barely a question asked. A good friend even wondered aloud after getting his MDiv if he should pursue an MBA to complete his preparation for ministry!

## *People seem to be longing for a more organic approach to life—even church life.*

We did not find the business/church growth model to be par-ticularly helpful. We wondered if there was a different metaphor. We researched, tested, and lived out our discoveries in our lives and in our business. When we tried sharing our insights with the congregations with whom we worked, however, we found that church growth practices were so entrenched that proposing a different process of thought was met with great opposition. Transition in a church setting seemed almost impossible.

It is our hope that those days are over. People seem to be longing for a more organic approach to life—even church life. Along the way I have met many leaders who are tired of the false promises made by the latest fad program. In our desire to help people with their lives and answer the question of *how*, we program community, which sometimes harms more than it helps. We are discovering that it is more helpful to nurture environments where spontaneous community can emerge.

---

*Praxis without thoughtfulness*
*is functional fantasy.*

---

We began our business hoping for a more organic foundation for growing a successful company. After fifteen years of living this way of life, I'm just now becoming comfortable with writing about organic order. Some books are written from the finish; they share the conclusions from the landing point. Others share an idea and a process from the point of conception. This book is written somewhere between the two. These are thoughts collected along our journey thus far.

I can't offer a neat and tidy answer to *how*, but I do think we can discover a lot from observation. Healthy observation combined with curiosity can lead to the development of practical insights. Praxis without thoughtfulness is functional fantasy.

This book will give you a framework for shifting your thinking. My work is informed by the architectural research of Christopher Alexander and his coauthors in *The Oregon Experiment*. Alexander and his team have influenced the way architects think about their practice. I expand on their studies and describe characteristics of environments where communities spontaneously live.

Another influence has been our friend and mentor Kennon Callahan. Sara and I owe him much for the rich sharing of his body of work on leadership. Our lives have been shaped by him.

In *The Search to Belong*, I discussed the organic patterns people use to develop a whole, healthy sense of belonging. Here in these pages, we continue the conversation. I introduce tools to develop an organic environment where community and belonging can emerge. I ask you to leave behind, as best you can, preconceived ideals—presumptions of knowing what's best.

This book will not build an argument from chapter to chapter. It is more like a mobile. Each chapter is independent in the sense that each has a self-contained message. Each chapter is dependent in the sense that each one is richer in the context of the other chapters. Each chapter provides some balance to the other chapters to keep the mobile swinging freely and in harmony as a whole. You can read them in an order that makes

> *When we look for tools and techniques, which are part of the How? question, we preempt other kinds of learning. In a sense, if we want to know what really works, we must carefully decide which are the right questions for this moment. Picking the right question is the beginning of action on what matters, and this is what works. This is how we name the debate, by the questions we pursue, for all these questions are action steps. Good questions work on us, we don't work on them. They are not a project to be completed but a doorway opening onto a greater depth of understanding, action that will take us into being more fully alive.[2]*
> —Peter Block, *The Answer to How Is Yes*

sense to you; I have organized them in a sequence that makes sense to me.

I invite you to observe nature, think organically, hone your wisdom, and begin to ponder the pursuit of the profound questions of community before rushing to answer *how* too soon.

# 1

# ORGANIC ORDER

*synchronized life*
**moving from master plan to organic order**

**A**s I settled in at thirty thousand feet, I noticed the young woman seated next to me slowly scanning a brochure. I discreetly tried to see what she was reading. The brochure advertised a seminar titled "New Watercolor Techniques for a Digital Environment."

I was keenly interested. I work in fine art. I am also a graphic artist, and I often work in a digital environment. The idea of mixing fine art with digital art piqued my curiosity.

The woman read the first page, then flipped to the second, then went back to page one. She turned the paper over and viewed the back, then opened it again and read the center section. As she made her way through the brochure a fifth time, I caught a glimpse of her photo.

Surprised, I started to say something, excited at the possibility of a rich conversation about art. The look on her face stopped me. Her expression was numb. As her hands massaged the brochure, her eyes and mind were somewhere else.

I glanced over again, careful not to stare. What were her thoughts? Was she nervous about the seminar? The brochure caught my attention once more; this time I noticed the date. She was returning; the seminar was over.

A wave of sympathy swept over me as I thought of ways the event could have been a disaster for her. I remembered times when I had boarded a plane excited about the scheduled engagement, only to return home deflated by the experience. Finally I spoke.

"You're an artist?"

She woke from her reverie and smiled at me. "Yes, I am," she replied.

"I noticed your photo on the brochure."

"Yes."

"So how did it go?"

She perked up. "It went really well."

"Great!" I said.

She came alive for the next few minutes as she shared how the seminar had exceeded her expectations and how she had helped most of the participants move their painting competencies forward.

She told me about new techniques she had discovered and explained the processes that led her to these discoveries. It was fun to see how excited she was.

"This is great stuff," I told her. "You've already helped me with my own work. But I'm a little confused. Before we began our conversation, you seemed upset, maybe unsure. Did something happen that caused you to question the success of the seminar?"

"Well . . ." She glanced again at the brochure.

"Do you mind my asking what happened?"

After a pause, she began. "The fact is, for about 90 percent of the participants, our time together was a process of learning. They came expecting to learn. And almost all of them were excited to share their own techniques, too.

"But I was not prepared for the other 10 percent. These people expected me to deliver a 'checklist/bullet-point/how-to plan' on watercolor painting. It caught me by surprise, and it distracted me from much of what I'd planned to do.

"They didn't want me to help them become artists. It was

more like they expected me to teach them how to manufacture art. I don't even know what that means."

I knew her confusion all too well.

When I was a boy, I started showing an interest in art. My parents often found me with pencil and paper, drawing anything and everything I could bring to mind. The front of the refrigerator door filled quickly with pieces I had completed.

I remember one Christmas in particular when I experienced the same disappointment that puzzled this young teacher. Because I had started to show a growing competency in art, my family encouraged me by giving me supplies and instructional books. The more presents I opened, the more excited I became.

---

*"They expected me to teach them how to manufacture art. I don't even know what that means."*

---

My expectations ran high when we arrived at Grandma's house. In her own way my grandmother was an artist. I just knew Grandma would give me presents selected with the wisdom and insight of a fellow artist!

The first gift came: brushes. Then the second: a large, rectangular box. I couldn't suppress my excitement. This would be the gift that would set me on the path of *Artist*. I unwrapped that present like a ravenous dog devouring a bowl of food, all the while composing in my mind the wonderful acceptance speech I would give to honor this gift and my hopeful future.

And then, there it was: a paint-by-numbers kit. I was shocked into silence.

Grandma kept looking at me as only grandmothers can, eyes full of love, a voice full of tenderness: "Now you can paint beautiful paintings."

Beautiful paintings! What did she think of the ones I had already done? Weren't they beautiful? Weren't they art? Her gift told me that in her mind I was no artist at all. I was just a little boy trying on a new hobby. Maybe if I could learn to follow somebody else's plan, I could produce "beautiful paintings."

It is not true that an artist is someone who manufactures art. An artist is someone who enables art to emerge from a canvas—someone who has the strengths, competencies, and patience to bring that miracle into being.

> *An artist is someone who enables art to emerge from a canvas.*

Art is not formulaic, like a paint-by-numbers kit. It has life. It is viewed and appreciated. It moves and inspires. It invites participation, intermingling its own story with those of its observers.

Some of the participants in the young woman's seminar believed that art could be created through an assembly line, *master plan* approach. They focused on the result, not on the becoming. They likely produced something more craft than art.

When it comes to our own lives, we want to be works of art—individually created and unique. We are living beings, and living beings cannot be manufactured on an assembly line, like a paint-by-numbers kit. Our souls long to be nourished with the life that emerges from *becoming*.

Shaping an environment where people naturally connect is

> *In musical compositions,*
> *so long as we hear merely single tones, we do not hear music.*
> *Hearing music depends on the reception of the in-between of the tones,*
> *of their placing and of their spacing.*
>
> *In writing, a knowledge of spelling has nothing to do with an*
> *understanding*
> *of poetry.*
>
> *Equally, a factual identification of colors within a given painting*
> *has nothing to do with a sensitive seeing*
> *nor with an understanding of the color action within the painting. . . .*
>
> *Our concern is the interaction of color; that is, seeing*
> *what happens between colors. . . .*
>
> *Colors present themselves in continuous flux, constantly related to*
> *changing neighbors and changing conditions.*[1]
>
> —Josef Albers, *Interaction of Color*

more like creating art than manufacturing a product. It marks a major shift: from programming community (i.e., following a *master plan*) to using principles of *organic order* to develop an environment where community can emerge.

Organic community has the human complexities that promote artistry over mechanics. In our worship of "how-to" pragmatism, we have in some cases treated the church as an object and programmed the life out of it. It would do us well to remember that our job is to help people with their lives rather than build infrastructures that help institutions stay alive. Sometimes we focus so much on building a "healthy church" that we forget to tend to the health of people.

Healthy environments are vital—alive. They are not inanimate—dead. When places encourage community to emerge spontaneously, they have motion, emotion, and a living spirit. The goal is not to manufacture community, nor is the goal to build programs. The hope is to watch living community emerge naturally and to collaborate with its environment in helpful, healthy ways.

The difference between a paint-by-numbers kit and the blank canvas of an artist is the difference between master plan and organic order. In short, master plan tries to manufacture life, whereas organic order is an invitation to live.

## *Master Plan:* Community Based on Programming

By "master plan," I mean a specific kind of plan. I'm not suggesting we throw out plans or planning, just *master* planning. Master plans describe a specific color and numbering system and then instruct you to paint inside the lines. Master plans intend to control the future. Master plans provide specific answers to future questions that have not yet been asked—that may *never* be asked. A master plan does not allow for flexibility, uncertainty, or serendipity—ingredients of the "aha" moment.

*Master plans intend to control the future.*

A master plan is an adopted instrument of policy intended to control individual acts. Architect Christopher Alexander and his colleagues, in their landmark book *The Oregon Experiment*, describe the master plan of a city in this way: it is "intended to coordinate the many hundreds of otherwise independent acts of building."[2] It is an attempt to infuse an environment with a controlled system.

As such, a master plan is often a welcome friend.

With a master plan, the future seems safe, less messy, less chaotic. People settle in and obey the master plan, trusting that it will bring a future unburdened by anxieties and complexities. They are often disappointed.

Again, Christopher Alexander and company:

> [T]he existence of a master plan alienates the users. . . . After all, the very existence of a master plan means, by definition, that the members of the community can have little impact on the future shape of their community, because most of the important decisions have already been made. In a sense, under a master plan people are living with a frozen future, able to affect only relatively trivial details. When people lose the sense of responsibility for the environment they live in, and realize that they are merely cogs in someone else's machine, how can they feel any sense of identification with the community, or any sense of purpose there?
>
> Second, neither the users nor the key decision makers can visualize the actual implications of the master plan.[3]

Those developing the master plan freeze their hopes for the future in *the plan*. This is not a vicious act. Indeed, those developing the master plan are likely to see it as a generous act—the gift of passing on their team's wisdom, spirit, and hope.

However, the plan was created in the present, which will soon become the past, and so the plan straitjackets those who will use it in the future. Master plans might work if we had the ability to foresee the future, but we do not. We barely know what we know today, let alone tomorrow.

A master plan "can create a totality, but not a whole. It can create totalitarian order, but not organic order," write the authors of *The Oregon Experiment*.[4] Master plans "are too rigid; they cannot easily adapt to the natural and unpredictable changes that inevitably arise in the life of a community."[5] Master plans and "totalitarian order" may be appropriate when it comes to manufacturing cars, refrigerators, and other inanimate objects. Vehicles produced by master plans are more economical, easier to maintain, and less expensive to repair than an exotic, hand-built one-off.

But developing something with life, such as community, requires the flexibility of organic order.

Living things yearn for wholeness, not for totality.

## *Organic Order:* Community Based on Environment

Essentially, master plans are maps that mix things that already exist with things that "ought" to exist. Master plans use the language of "ought" and "should," language that points to the future in a rigid, predetermined way. The problem is that "ought" and "should" are often interpreted to mean "must!" This future—the plan—*must* be protected and preserved.

Master plans embalm embryos; they are a form of cryogenics.

Organic order, on the other hand, does not use a language of "oughts" and "shoulds." It presents a language of possibilities.

When people are planning a new initiative (at church, for example), they often start with the question "Where are we headed?" This question prompts a point-to-point totalitarian master plan of the future. The question "Where are we headed?" is always answered with some form of "There!"

From this question we develop a plan that is both too precise and not precise enough.[6] It is too precise because it describes the future in specific detail, as a point or place. Our plan says,

"This is what the future will look like, and this is where we will end up if we follow this plan." At the same time, the plan is not precise enough because it cannot deliver the guidance necessary to answer questions as yet unasked, but which inevitably will arise.

---

*Master plans embalm embryos; they are a form of cryogenics.*

---

When we plan, it is helpful to begin with a horizon in view instead of a specific point. This is a more organic concept of planning for the future. It is not very helpful to speak in terms of going from "here" to "there," because we as living creatures need the freedom to end up somewhere else.

Besides, in my experience, *there* is hardly ever better than *here*.

"Begin with the end in mind," we hear people say. This is totalitarian fantasy. How many times have you arrived at the place you planned to go only to find an uncertainty you did not expect?

Take Kip, for example. He is in every way a conspicuous success. Married to his high school sweetheart for thirty years, Kip retired at fifty-five, and he and his wife have seen much of the world. Their two boys finished near the top of their classes at Ivy League schools; one is a physician and the other is a lawyer. Kip followed his plan—*he made it.*

And yet there he sat, in my office, bewildered and asking questions—big questions.

"What do you say to a man," Kip asked, "who has everything he wants except the one thing he wants most?"

As we puzzled through his question, it became clear that Kip knew where he was going, but it never occurred to him that this "where" may not deliver the "what" he was looking for. Kip had found totality but not wholeness.

When planning a new initiative, I prefer to ask, "What are we hoping for?" Your answer to this question, whatever it might be, will serve as an organic guide. Most likely, the answer will allow enough flexibility to deal with future questions as they emerge and the guiding principles to answer those questions more effectively.

---

*Our focus should be on the journey,*
*not the destination.*

---

"Where are we headed?" is a destination-based question. "Where" necessitates that we respond with a place or point. "What are we hoping for?" is a journey-based question. "What" asks for an answer that will help with the journey—*where*-ever it may take us. "What" also helps us recognize the substance of the journey, not merely the direction or destination of the journey. We often have little control over precise direction. We do have some control over the substance of the journey.

In golf, when learning to putt well, you first concentrate on how fast and how far the ball travels (the journey) when you strike it with the putter. Direction and destination are secondary to getting a feel for the speed and distance of a putt. You have some control over how hard you hit the ball. You don't have precise control over the ball's direction or destination. There are too many variables: the grain of the grass, footprints from other players, minute clumps of sand, undetected undulation in the surface of the green, wind, and so on.

When you understand speed and distance, your understanding of direction and destination will follow. Even then, an excellent putt does not always go into the cup. Tiger Woods has commented many times that he was putting well, but "they just didn't go in the hole."

Our focus should be on the journey, not the destination. When planning for organic community, the question that will move us forward is "What are we hoping for?" not "Where are we headed?"

It is a search for wholeness, not for totalitarian order.

This is not a call for "come what may" leadership and ministry. There is a difference between being *organic* and seeking *organic order*. It is the difference between an infant's response to her body's need to release waste and her father's need to do the same. If her father were to respond to this need in a strictly organic way, he too would need diapers. Thankfully he has developed an order for an organic process.

"Eliminating the [master] plan is not a call for chaos," writes Christopher Alexander and his collaborators. "Rather it is an attempt to overcome the difficulties inherent in this way of ordering the environment: the impossibility of making accurate predictions about the future needs and resources; the ignorance of the more minute relationships between places [and people] which are not prescribed in the plan; the insensitivity of the plan to the ongoing needs of users; and the alienating quality of the plan as an administrative device."[7]

It is not enough to simply become more organic. Seek organic order.

For example, I'm not asking you to dismantle your small group program. I am asking you to rethink using small groups as the master plan for people's lives. As I explain in *The Search to Belong*, I like small groups. I question, however, the manner in which they are promoted and structured. At their best, small groups supply an organic-ordered environment for *some* people in *some* seasons of their lives to grow their sense of healthy community and belonging. At their worst, small groups deliver a manufactured environment that is promoted for *all* people and for *every* season of life.

Alexander writes the following about architectural master plans, but the same is true for people: "The master plan seems to suggest that the buildings [people] which fill in the slots can have any shape at all. It does not specify the critical relationships which buildings [people] must have in common, to make them functioning members of the same family."[8]

In my book *The Search to Belong*, I call for practitioners to make the shift from programmer (master planner) to environmentalist (one who follows the principles of organic order to create and shape environments). I have spoken with many who are intrigued by this call, but questions emerge: "What guidelines can you use as an environmentalist?" "How do you measure success?" This book, *Organic Community*, provides a framework for a mental and practical shift. It is intended for those who daringly make the move to environmentalist.

Nine organizational tools will help you discover whether

> *If people cannot even understand the concrete and human implications of a master plan after studying it, then it is extremely dangerous and foolish to rely on such a plan as a guide to future development. Whatever tool is used to guide development must be a tool which people can understand in concrete and human terms, and in terms of their everyday experience.*[9]
> —Christopher Alexander and others,
> *The Oregon Experiment*

you are following a master plan approach or an organic order approach. The chart below contrasts the two approaches.

| Organizational Tool | Master Plan (Programmer) | Organic Order (Environmentalist) |
|---|---|---|
| Patterns | *Prescriptive* | *Descriptive* |
| Participation | *Representative* | *Individual* |
| Measurement | *Bottom Line* | *Story* |
| Growth | *Bankrupt* | *Sustainable* |
| Power | *Positional* | *Revolving* |
| Coordination | *Cooperation* | *Collaboration* |
| Partners | *Accountability* | *Edit-ability* |
| Language | *Noun-centric* | *Verb-centric* |
| Resources | *Scarcity* | *Abundancy* |

Discover with me how shifting from a master plan understanding to an organic order approach can help create environments where people naturally connect—indeed become—organic community.

# 2 PATTERNS

*spatial observation*
**moving from prescriptive to descriptive**

**P**atterns are integral to our lives. They protect us, help us organize what we do from day to day, and even entertain us. Most of the time, we don't even think about them. We simply absorb them.

When we see a man coming toward us in the distance, we observe the pattern of his walk and know instantly that he is a good friend and not someone intending to do us harm. When we wake up in the morning, our first thought may be *What day is it?* Weekdays tend to follow one pattern; weekends another. We hear three or four notes of a melody and we begin to sing along.

Patterns, as organizational tools, can be prescriptive or descriptive. Master plans tend to follow *prescriptive* patterns. Prescriptive patterns are "prescribed"; they are specific, rigid, and regular. A physician dictates which medication you should use, how often you should take it, and for how long. A general aviation pilot knows to follow a basic airport-traffic pattern when an airport has no air traffic control tower. The patient gets better; collisions are minimized. Sometimes prescriptive patterns are good and necessary.

But when we talk about community, prescriptive patterns are limited in their capacity to be helpful. Forcing connections among people is awkward and uncomfortable.

Organic order is strengthened by *descriptive* patterns. Descriptive patterns have an expressive, evocative, and eloquent spirit.

*For the past half-century, these terms [prescriptive and descriptive] have served as useful labels for two contrasting approaches to the study of grammar and usage and especially to the teaching of these matters. They have also long served as epithets in the recurrent name-calling that quarreling over correctness, appropriateness, and permissiveness in language seems to elicit.*

*The terms represent polar values: (1) A descriptive approach to language describes in full detail precisely how we use that language. The chief values of this approach are accuracy and an unretouched picture of usage, warts and all. (2) A prescriptive approach insists that however many variables might be found, there are better and worse choices; it will specify at least which is most appropriate, more likely which is acceptable, or, in its most rigorous application, which is correct. Clearly, the prescriptive approach is easier to teach—there is always one right answer; the descriptive approach may offer several possible answers, each appropriate in one or another context. . . .*

*The problem is that a simplistic "correct" answer may seem helpful, but often when it appears to contradict users' experience, they will either shrug off the prescription or find themselves unable to accept it. For example: to say succinctly that irregardless is not a word or at least that it ought to be treated as though it were not a word, is prescriptive. The "rule" being promulgated is: Don't use irregardless; pretend it doesn't exist, because, in fact, it's not in Standard English.*

*But, in fact, that's not true. It is a word, and therefore it is in the dictionaries; many people use it, including some who in other respects speak Standard English. A descriptive account of the word will show who uses it and when, where, and why. Irregardless, it turns out, occurs regularly in Common and Vulgar English, but in Standard its only acceptable use is jocular. A descriptive account will end by pointing out that the inadvertent use of irregardless in Standard English can be a shibboleth.*

*The prescriptive commentator then impatiently inquires, Why all the fuss? Why pussyfoot about? Just tell the world not to use irregardless—that's simple, sound, and teachable. The descriptive commentator will offer at least two objections: (1) The word may be Substandard now, but you can't be sure it won't change in status. In fact it may be in the process of such change even now: it may be fading to an obsolete status (in which case we can stop talking about it), or it may someday become Standard. (2) Even more important, sometimes Standard speakers do use irregardless; the issue is where and how.*[1]

—Kenneth G. Wilson, *The Columbia Guide to Standard American English*

They *describe* reality. They don't *force* it. We discover descriptive patterns through observation, as they emerge.

---

## *Forcing connections among people is awkward and uncomfortable.*

---

My mother-in-law, Autumn, remembers fondly the gift that her mother, Ruth, gave her after each of her three children's births. Yes, Ruth had come for several days to give Autumn time to recuperate, help with the laundry, the meals, and so forth, but primarily Ruth had come to give Autumn an opportunity to get to know each newborn.

"Mom let me spend entire days just watching Lila, Eric, and Sara. I got to know how each one slept, how each one breathed, what their cries were like. In short, I learned what was usual for them. That helped me recognize what was unusual for them."

Autumn was observing the descriptive patterns of her children's lives.

Wisely, Autumn did not try to turn these descriptive patterns into prescriptive patterns. She did not force Eric, who was born four years after Lila, to follow the same routines Lila had followed.

Lila was one to fall asleep early and sleep through the night. Eric, even as a toddler, never went to bed before midnight, and he rarely needed more than four or five hours of sleep. Sara, born five years after Eric, had her own unique patterns as well.

We instinctively know that we must raise our children as individuals. We know that we must observe and be attuned to the uniqueness of each person. Why then do we so frequently reverse the process and adopt models and programs that force prescriptive patterns onto our congregations?

## *Where We Get into Trouble*

Prescriptive patterns rarely start out as such. They are usually rooted in descriptive patterns. We see or experience a pattern that "works," and then we assume that if we repeat the pattern exactly, we can manufacture the same result. This works almost well enough often enough to convince us that it could work all the time.

Think of some movements that have promised that a specific pattern will work for every participant, for all time. One that comes to my mind is the labor movement. Unions promised their members that they would be "set for life." Great pressure was put on every eligible employee to join. Most did, and for many years unions and their members flourished. As of this writing, however, union membership is declining. Globalization, the growing service economy, Reagan's handling of the air traffic controllers' strike, and other such factors have influenced the current generation of workers, many of whom have determined that there just isn't much benefit to joining. The landscape has changed. The workplace environment is different.

Similar promises abound in religious circles. Even though the fine print of just about every "church growth" book suggests that readers should adopt only the principles that work for their particular situations, some congregational leaders take a prescriptive stance and insist on taking the author's model (which *describes* a pattern that worked for the *author's* congregation) and duplicating it.

In my short time on earth, I've witnessed or participated in various church models: the purpose-driven church model, the cell church model, the house church model, the seeker-sensitive model, the servant-evangelism model, the natural church model, the connecting church model, and on and on. And I'm not that old!

*Organic order suggests there are **many** patterns we can use to connect to God and others.*

These are all wonderful, descriptive, organic patterns that worked—they worked with *those* participants; they worked in *those* communities; they worked in *those* environments. We get into trouble when we think someone else's model will work *exactly as described* with *our* participants, in *our* communities, in *our* environments. We turn a descriptive, organic order pattern into a forced, prescriptive, master plan pattern. Participants begin to feel like they are nameless soldiers marching in lockstep, turning right or left at the command of the officer.

Organic order suggests there are *many* patterns we can use to connect to God and others. All faces follow a pattern, but few, if any, are identical. Patterns do not produce clones.

## Patterns of Belonging

Many churches have adopted the small group as their favorite community model. They suggest that a sense of belonging is guaranteed by participating in a small group. They have prescribed a specific pattern that worked for some and, they now believe, will work for every person, for all time.

Indeed, small groups are *a* pattern of effective connection. We see this in the lives of many people. But we cross a line when we attempt to prescribe small groups as *the* answer for everyone and for every season of a person's life. Inevitably, prescriptive language creeps in, and we assign a judgment, saying they are "a good" or "the best" way to get to know God. I've even heard people say small groups are "the *only* way to get plugged in."

In *The Search to Belong*, I discuss four descriptive patterns of belonging. These patterns emerged from my study of Edward Hall's theory of *proxemics*, which is his term "for the inter-related observations and theories of man's use of space."[2] He concluded that people use specific spatial references to develop communication and culture.

Hall proposed four spatial references: public, social, personal, and intimate. I believe that we use this same set of spatial references to gather the connections we need in order to experience belonging and a sense of community. We have significant public belonging, significant social belonging, significant personal belonging, and significant intimate belonging. And there is a pattern to how we use each of these relational spaces.

I have observed that healthy people live a pattern of connection that looks much like the chart on the next page. The pattern in the chart implies that we have more significant public belongings than significant social belongings. Public belonging occurs when people connect through an outside influence. Fans of a certain sports team, for example, experience a sense of community because they cheer for the same team. They wear official garb, buy special broadcast viewing privileges, and stay up late or get up early just to see the results of the game. These public belongings have great significance in our lives.

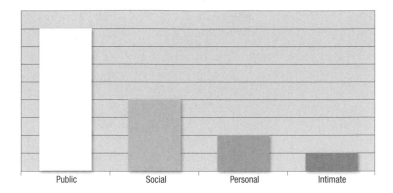

The chart also indicates that we have more significant social belongings than we do personal. Social belonging occurs when we share "snapshots" of ourselves—small vignettes that reveal a bit about us. The phrases "first impression" and "best foot forward" refer to this spatial reference. You belong socially to your favorite bank teller, your pharmacist, or some of the people with whom you work.

Social belonging is important for many reasons. I'll suggest three. First, it provides the space for "neighbor" relationships. A neighbor is someone with whom you feel comfortable exchanging small favors.

Second, social belongings provide a safe "selection space" or "sorting space" among those with whom you may want to develop a "deeper" relationship. In social space we provide the information that helps others decide whether they connect with us. We give and receive just enough information to decide to keep this person in social space or to move them to another space.

Third, social space is the place where we practice telling who we are. As we share snapshots of ourselves, we often select a picture that is more likely to connect with the other person. For example, when I'm talking to musicians, I let them know

I'm a guitar player. I don't normally do that when I'm mingling with a roomful of small group pastors.

When we have a number of social spaces, we have multiple opportunities to share snapshots. The more opportunities we have, the more snapshots we can share. This in turn helps us understand the whole of who we are, what I call "social self-talk," which is the process of sharing snapshots of who we are with ourselves. Rarely do we share these with anyone else. In fact, many are negative—*I'm fat, I'm ugly, I'm not likeable, I'm* _____.

Sharing a variety of snapshots with numerous people in all kinds of circumstances strengthens our self-image—the whole of who we are. It makes it easier to confess to ourselves that we are actually complex and multifaceted.

The person with limited opportunities to connect in social space can share only a few snapshots of herself, omitting some that might be quite significant to her and interesting to another person. Plus, with limited social space connections, our self-talk takes on too much importance. We start to believe the negative things we say to ourselves, whether or not they are real or true, giving them much more importance than they should have.

The patterns of belonging represented by the bar graph show that healthy community comes when we have more significant personal belongings than intimate. In personal space, we share private (not naked) experiences, feelings, and thoughts. We call those with whom we connect in personal space our "close friends." They know more about us than an acquaintance knows, yet not so much that they feel uncomfortable.

In intimate space, we share our most closely held experiences, thoughts, and feelings. These people know all there is to know about us; with them, we are "naked and unashamed." Healthy persons reveal that they have very few significant intimate belongings. Thus, it is not true that the more intimate connections you have, the healthier you are or will become.

The four spaces describe an organic order, descriptive pattern for helping people with their search for community. We do not experience belonging in only one or two of these spaces. All four contribute to our health and connectedness. We need connections in all four.

## *The Four Spaces Are Descriptive, Not Prescriptive*

I've watched good people try to help others by prescribing a specific set of behaviors, hoping to reproduce the same result over and over. Although well-meaning, the prescriptors end up manipulating and guilting people into situations that ultimately deliver alienation instead of help. Imagine a doctor prescribing for Bob a drug to which he is allergic simply because the same drug worked well for Suzie. Prescriptions are by their own nature designed for particular individuals with particular problems and particular strengths. In fact, the medical community goes to great lengths to tell us not to share prescriptions because doing so could be very dangerous.

So I remind you that the four spaces represent organic order, descriptive patterns. They describe how people organize their belongings. Some individuals, when first learning about the four spaces, try to turn this descriptive pattern into a prescriptive path. I hear: "We'll have people start in public space, then move them to social space, then move them to public space, and finally to intimate space." The speaker implies that congregants won't meet God until they've crossed the threshold of intimate space.

Churches sometimes ask individuals to make intimate con-nections they are not ready to make. An intimate connection with God, an intimate connection with the stranger across the small group circle, an intimate connection with a discipler/mentor—these are all well intended but may not be what *every* person needs at *that* time in his or her life.

This "encouragement" may also be quietly reinforced within church leadership structures. Perhaps we've successfully forced everyone into some form of a small group. This in itself might be okay if we recognize that many kinds of groupings can serve the same role as "small groups." Instead, the pressure continues when small group leaders are told that if intimate connections are not taking place within their groups, their groups are fail-ures. We need to bear in mind that the most accurate word to describe the process of forcing intimate connection is *rape*.

A healthier approach might be to provide help within spaces that are appropriate for an individual's situation. Mary might find significant help by simply entering our church's public space (the sanctuary, for example) and going home. She may not engage at all in social, personal, or intimate spaces. We need to be comfortable accepting that *that one event* may be the whole of Mary's experience with us. She might see it as a significant, helpful event. We might see it only as a "good first step."

How open to and observant of descriptive patterns are we? Do we recognize the uniqueness of our participants, of our community, of our environment?

My wife and I travel a lot. When at home, we work till early evening. Thus, we eat out often. We try to choose restaurants with healthy options.

From time to time, I ask servers to modify an offering on their menu. I never request an extreme modification. I may simply want to substitute a soup instead of a salad, or a fresh vegetable in place of french fries. What I request I usually see elsewhere on the menu.

So I am always dumbfounded when my request is answered with a perfunctory "no." The server says "no." Not: "I'll have to charge you more for that substitution." Not: "We could offer you this instead." But rather just "no."

---

*Churches sometimes ask individuals to make intimate connections they are not ready to make.*

---

Sometimes the same thing happens with our small groups. A small group participant or leader may ask the person "in charge" if the group could divert from a curriculum, or schedule alternative meeting times or places. Often the request is borne of recognition of a descriptive pattern in the group's life.

Too often, however, the request is greeted with "no." This prescriptive stance results in one of several outcomes: the group disbands; the group continues as it was, but now has a simmering level of discontent; or, if courage prevails, the group goes "underground." It simply disregards the prescription and follows the descriptive, organic pattern that works for its members.

Let's not force our groups to go "underground." Instead, think about being open to descriptive patterns of organic order rather than implementing rigid molds of prescriptive master plans. Create environments and spaces that encourage the patterns of belonging and allow people to connect naturally in all kinds of ways.

Begin to see *all* connections as significant. Don't use a master plan, prescriptive approach. It is not necessary to process people through the spaces 1-2-3-4 to get them to "important," "real," or "authentic" (intimate) relationships.

---

*Create environments and spaces that encourage the patterns of belonging and allow people to connect naturally in all kinds of ways.*

---

*All* of these spaces are important, real, and authentic in people's lives. As we validate the patterns each person counts as valid, we will begin to help people with their lives.

Games and melodies all follow patterns. Yet each has a spirit of individuality. Who would want to play in or watch a basketball tournament if every game was the same? Who would want to play a piece of music if you weren't permitted to add your own expression? Even jugglers, who seemingly follow a rigid pattern, use improvisation and creativity in their routines.

The same is true of our belongings. People are not looking to experience sameness—the product of a program that sends each person through a step-by-step assembly line of so-called belonging. People know intuitively that all of our connections follow patterns, yet connections have a spirit of individuality too; no two connections are exactly the same, nor should they be. We need to encourage patterns that make room for individualized connections.

As we evaluate how to go about creating environments in which organic community can emerge, we may consider evaluating the way we use the organizational tool of patterns. Do we use a master plan to prescribe the way people *should* belong? Or do we—with relaxed intentionality—create environments that validate the patterns people naturally use to connect?

# 3

# PARTICIPATION

*responsible anarchy*
moving from representative to individual

*oken woman. Token black.* In the 1960s and '70s, these phrases were thrown around liberally, and always with disdain. Companies felt forced to hire "token women," and they were resentful, thinking they were putting someone into a position who wasn't qualified for it. The "token women" were angry because they believed they were not hired on merit.

The same was true for African-American students in universities and colleges. They felt like "token blacks," accepted to fill affirmative action quotas rather than because they were promising students.

## Nobody wants to be a token anything.

Obviously, my statements are vast oversimplifications of complex issues, and because I've talked about "token women" and "token blacks" as groups and not as individuals, I run the risk of seeming like I'm going against what I present in the following pages. But the point I'm trying to make is this: Nobody wants to be a token anything.

Surely tokenism doesn't happen anymore, does it? And certainly not in church!

As Sara and I entered the auditorium where our worship services were held, we were given the customary program that included the order of worship and several loose-leaf announcements. I sat and quickly glanced over the printed material I was given while taking intermittent breaks to scan the congregation for friends.

This particular week there were more loose-leaf announcements than usual. I discovered that this was "Volunteer Sunday." There was a page with an overview of the specific program the church was going to use to enlist more volunteers, one with a survey that each of us was to complete about our specific S.H.A.P.E. (Spiritual gifts, Heart, Abilities, Personality, Experience), a list of all the ministries through which we could help the church, and a sheet that invited us to indicate where we would like to serve. The last paper had a section at the bottom of the page where we were to sign a commitment statement. I remember thinking, *This looks like good stuff.*

The worship service was focused. The sermon pointed to the scriptural mandate to serve, the benefits of serving, and the needs of the church that would only be met if "I" volunteered. It was challenging, logical, and reasonable. The entire service was motivating and inspiring.

On the way home, I went over the material again, trying to give the process some of my best thought. I was excited to go through the S.H.A.P.E. survey. I looked forward to gaining some clarity and insight into how I was made to serve.

Following the instructions later that evening, I read the list of possibilities and tried to match the discoveries of the S.H.A.P.E. survey with the available opportunities. I was genuinely excited about finding a place—my place—at our church.

Monday morning I got up early enough to look over the sheets one more time and then drove them by the church building on my way to the rest of the day's activities. I could hardly wait to receive the phone call asking me to help and giving me instructions on where I was needed the most. The first day came and went, as did the first week. No call. *Maybe they're just inundated with so many responses that they haven't been able to process mine yet*, I thought.

The next Sunday I expected that maybe one of the pastors or ministry leaders would say something to me. Not a word. By the end of the first month, I had grown disappointed. By the end of six months, I was cynical. Feeling unwanted, Sara and I eventually searched for another congregation.

I wish I could say that this only happened one time. But I can't. To be truthful, something like this has happened at almost every church Sara and I have attended. A collective "want ad" is placed in the church bulletin. An ambitious master plan is rolled out. We look for a match, and we fill out the survey as best we can, but we quickly see that the gifts we have aren't on the list provided. And even though we offer our gifts in other ways, we are really only asked to help in ways the church *wants* us to help—filling a spot, not really finding our place. We end up saying, "We just don't fit here."

*Many church leaders have spent too much time on the art of **getting** people to participate and too little time trying to understand **how** people participate.*

I have discovered that we're not alone. There are many who have been discarded when their "shape" didn't match the "shape" of the congregation.

People long to participate. They are looking for their place, a place that feels like home. However, many times there's a disconnect between longing to participate and actually participating.

How do we close the gap? Is it a matter of motivation? A matter of timing? Whatever the reason, one observation is clear. Many church leaders have spent too much time on the art of *getting* people to participate and too little time trying to understand *how* people participate.

## How Do People Participate?

People want to participate in organic ways, not in "strategic" (master plan) ways. They really don't care about our strategies of participation; they are interested in the participation itself. *We* (leaders) are the ones excited about the strategies our thinking and hard work have produced. People look for place before purpose, which is to say they seek first to belong before helping to meet a goal.

Master plan thinking is principally concerned with accomplishment of the plan. Thus, leaders who rely on master plans invite people to participate in ways that will best serve the plan. They ask people to participate as representatives of this or that grouping—token this's or that's—hoping they will become part of a force that will accomplish the task.

In a master plan, people are objectified as commodities. We need a "Sunday school teacher." You are asked to fill that slot so there's a warm body in the room with preschoolers, not because you love three- and four-year-olds. We need a "parking lot attendant." You are asked to stand out in the bitter cold so there's no traffic jam between services, not because you know many of the people in the congregation by name and can greet them with a genuine, warm smile.

People are not looking to become "goods or services."

> *Whether they are women, minorities, people with handicaps, or the elderly, tokens are often treated as symbols or representatives of the marginal social group to which they belong. As a result, their thoughts, beliefs, and actions are likely to be taken as typical of all in their social group. . . . In short, the token is less an individual than a social category. . . .*
>
> *Tokens can never be seen as who they really are. They must always fight stereotypes and tailor their actions to the desires and tastes of others. We can see the self-fulfilling prophecy at work here. Stereotypical assumptions about what tokens "must be like" force them into playing limited and caricatured roles. This situation serves the interests of those in the dominant group, who can fall back on preexisting expectations and traditional behaviors.*[1]
>
> —David M. Newman, *Sociology*

In my observations of healthy, organic environments, I have noticed the following five elements:

- People participate as individuals, not as teams or groups.
- People participate in a decentralized, local way.
- People participate with the whole of their lives.
- People participate in a way that is congruous with the way they are asked.
- The aggregate of participation becomes "known" as the team or group acts, thinks, and makes decisions.

### People Participate as Individuals

Organic order invites participation in an individual way, not a representative way. The invitation is to act as an individual, with the good of the group in mind.

Think of a pickup basketball game. Captains pick their team-mates one by one. As they make their choices, they have a sense of what each individual can contribute. One captain asks Pete, DeShawn, Alex, and Michael to join. The opposing captain invites Marcus, Todd, Bobby, and Damon to the team. Each captain has a sense of each person's individual competencies and ability to play together. They do not make their selections by just saying I need a forward, I need a point guard, I need a center, and so on.

*As people participate as individuals, they feel free to act for the good of the group as a whole.*

Nor do they make their selections based on achieving diversity. Sometimes master plan thinking tries to make sure teams or groups are "diverse." As we look at a group, we might ask ourselves: Have we gathered a variety of ethnic, socio-economic, political, religious, and social backgrounds?

This smacks of tokenism.

We devise a small group of entrepreneurs. We assemble a group of teachers. We create a grouping of student athletes. These are not bad ideas—if we invite each person to participate because of who they are as individuals, rather than what they represent.

Diversity will be present in the group because we have invited individuals. We are honoring each person's uniqueness.

Another contrast between organic order thinking and master plan thinking is that organic order is concerned with the health of the individual before the health of the organization or the plan. It encourages and welcomes "responsible anarchy." What do I mean by this?

Simply: As people participate as individuals, they feel free to act for the good of the group as a whole.

As my wife and I discussed the concept of responsible anarchy, she stated: "Anarchy implies going against some institution or plan that is already in existence or power. Does that mean you're always over and against something? And how is responsible anarchy lived out when there is no master plan—nothing to 'go against'?"

I reminded her of a time that I thought she demonstrated responsible anarchy.

One Sunday I preached about Jesus's triumphal entry. One question I asked was, "Did Jesus instruct the disciples to steal the donkey?"

The practice of our Sunday morning adult Bible study is to spend the hour discussing the previous week's sermon. So the following week my question was a hot topic. And a more general follow-up question was posed: Would Jesus ever ask us to break one of God's commandments?

Several members of the class confidently answered no and the group moved on.

Sara couldn't let this rest.

"Can we go back to that last question?" she interrupted. "Two weeks ago, Hurricane Katrina hit. People were dying on sidewalks and bridges. If there was a woman at our feet, dehydrated, and a locked drugstore was right there on the corner with bottled water inside—are you saying that Jesus wouldn't want us to break in and steal that water? I think he would."

Discussion ensued immediately.

I remember Sara telling me that she didn't have a particularly strong opinion about the group's responses; she just didn't want people to give pat answers.

"I wanted them to really think about what they were saying," she said.

In some environments, such healthy disagreement would be shut down or discouraged.

We see this in our business. Our company has a sense of responsible anarchy. We are very organic. Almost all of our clients, however, are institutional (master plan based). Most are billion-dollar megacorporations, rife with policies and procedures.

Sometimes, in order to meet an impossible deadline, we ask them to consider circumventing one of their policies or procedures. We do not ask them to do anything illegal or inappropriate, just expedient.

For example, sometimes a client has an idea of how a process should be completed. Their collective thinking has determined the "best" way to complete the task. When we know of a more expedient way to do it, we speak up.

We have learned which clients are open to our suggestions and see them as offers of help. We have also discovered which clients prefer our silence. In general, our working relationships with the "open" clients are more collaborative and productive for both parties.

I am not advocating anarchy, only responsible anarchy.

There is considerable debate about what anarchy is. Some define it politically, describing chaos and attempts to overthrow persons in authority. Others define it in a social sense, and honor it as a healthy, almost utopian state of mutual respect and cooperation.

I am not talking about responsible anarchy as "going against" just for the sake of going against, or for the purpose of overthrowing or gaining power. Responsible anarchy is about acting for the good of the group. It helps protect against "group think." It is an anomaly that is responsible for keeping the group together while at the same time preserving the individuality of each person.

---

*Responsible anarchy . . . is an anomaly that is responsible for keeping the group together while at the same time preserving the individuality of each person.*

---

In *The World As I See It*, Albert Einstein wrote,

Only the individual can think, and thereby create new values for society—nay, even set up new moral standards to which the life of the community conforms. Without creative, independently thinking and judging personalities the upward development of society is as unthinkable as the development of the individual personality without the nourishing soil of the community.[2]

### People Participate in a Decentralized, Local Way

How open are you to allowing people to operate with autonomy? Are group members free to practice their gifts locally?

Sometimes we fall into the trap of using master plan thinking because we think it reduces risk, and this subconsciously makes us feel safer. Does it really?

People want to participate with some autonomy. In particular, people want to contribute specifically in the way they uniquely can, as individuals.

The key is, we (leaders) must measure what they do as valid.

When we limit people's involvement to only what *we* see or confine them to using only the methods *we* deem relevant, we pigeonhole them and close ourselves off to a wealth of possibilities. We also imply that we don't trust them.

---

## *People are not interested in hearing us tell them how they must participate.*

---

Yes, following this descriptive path (see chapter 2, "Patterns") may feel uncomfortable; we may not like this feeling of being "out of control." However, people are not interested in hearing us tell them how they must participate. Nor do they want us to consider what they offer to do as invalid because their gifts aren't "on our list." People would like the opportunity for their ideas, gifts, and personality to shape the group. They are interested in developing groups that make sense to them.

David Weinberger, in his book *Small Pieces Loosely Joined*, talks about Amazon.com and the Web:

> [The] Web consists of hundreds of millions of individuals. They are a mass, but each member is unique. Individuals write reviews. The massness of the individuals makes the aggregate of reviews useless. So Amazon captures summary information, 1–5 stars, from the mass of individual reviews. But because those numeric rankings slight the individual side of the Web, the site begins to star the individual reviewers—but by using the masses' review of the reviewers as its criterion. And so on. One can almost feel the breeze from the pendulum as it swings this way or

that: massness, individuality, massness, individuality. And, most important, a new relationship between them: the Web consists of a mass that refuses to lose its individual faces. . . .

On the Web, each person is present only insofar as she has presented herself in an individual expression of her interests: many small faces, each distinct within the multitude.[3]

Autonomy doesn't mean solitude. Remember, by participating, people are searching for home. They are looking to find their place to connect and contribute with others—just not at the cost of losing their individuality.

## People Participate with the Whole of Their Lives

Participants bring with them the whole of their lives. No one participates from a blank slate. Instead of granting people the complexity due them, leaders often expect those who participate to be free of their own histories, detached from all that makes up their lives.

So instead of searching for ideal participants who are "perfect" for the job, look forward to people bringing the wealth of the whole of their lives with them and to the project. This is a blessing, not a detriment!

People also want what they are doing now to fit into the whole of their lives. Participation with the team is now and will be forever part of the story of their life. Encouraging autonomy helps them connect this project to their life in a way that makes sense for them.

People are not looking for their lives to be segmented into this and that category. People participate within the rhythm of the whole of their lives—past, present, and future.

### *People Participate in a Way That Is Congrous with the Way They Are Asked*

I've heard it said that when asking someone to participate, you should include in "the ask" two ingredients. One, you should include how their participation will directly benefit them. And two, you should include how their contribution will better the group. Basically, offering these two cost-benefits are a response to our misunderstanding that people generally operate from a position of "What's in it for me?"

*People . . . want to know that you have chosen them first and foremost because of **who they are**, not to fulfill a strategic master plan.*

I don't find this presumption to be true. Most people are not primarily selfish or self-serving. I do not see that people are asking, "What's in it for me?" Instead, they want to know, "*Why me?*" This is not a self-serving question. It is a self-identifying, individual question.

People participate as individuals. They are interested in why they—specifically—are being asked. They want to know that you have chosen them first and foremost because of *who they are*, not to fulfill a strategic master plan.

"Why me?" comes from a deep desire to live beyond one's self. A person wants to contribute in concrete ways, possibly in ways that *only he or she* could.

In our business, we have seen our company grow from three

of us—Sara, me, and our business partner—to a team of about fifty people nationwide.

Almost daily now, we receive unsolicited résumés and inquiries from individuals who are interested in working with us. The first question we ask ourselves is, "Is he or she the right person?" We are more concerned with hiring the right person than with hiring someone to fill a position (see chapter 6, "Power").

One day we received a call from "Jim," who was thinking of making a career change. "I can't think of anywhere else I'd rather work," Jim said.

We had developed a strong bond with Jim over the years. He had been a mentor to us, and we knew he was highly competent and shared our values. We were thrilled and honored that he would even consider working with us.

"Come in and let's talk," I said to him.

We met and explored several scenarios for working together. By the end of our visit, we were confident that Jim was the right person. Jim had a sense that we would be a good fit for him. He also knew that we had no "position" to offer him. We wanted to hire him, but there was no job to fall into; his responsibilities would be figured out as we went along, in a descriptive, organic way (see chapter 2, "Patterns").

For various reasons, Jim decided to stay with his employer. A few months later, he called again.

"Is that position still open?" he asked.

"Position? What position?" I said. "We wanted to hire you because of who you are. We don't have any position."

Jim is now on board, finding his place.

When I'm asked to join a team for a golf scramble, my first question is, "Why me?" Was I asked for my skills in driving the ball? For my putting and chipping skills? Or just for the fun I'll bring to the day? The same is true when we ask people to participate on a task team, a reading group, as a friend, in marriage, or a small group. "Why me?" is the first question (and it's not always verbalized).

---

*"Come after me, and I will make you*

*fishers of men" . . . is not*

*master plan language.*

---

Be prepared to know the answer to this question. Our answer cannot be organizationally driven. It cannot be group oriented. It cannot be responded to in the language of master plans. People are looking for answers that connect with them as individuals. They are looking for specific answers. Our responses will let them know that we have thought about them in specific ways. They are looking for us to answer with *their individual* "why," not our strategic, organizational "why."

"Come after me, and I will make you fishers of men" makes sense only in the context of asking fishermen to participate. It is not an "ask" for all individuals. It is not master plan language. It is individual and specific language. Jesus didn't ask all of the disciples to follow in this way. Only the fishermen were invited with this plea.

People are not looking for us to give a deeply personal or intimate answer to their "Why me?" question. Mostly they are looking for us to give a thoughtful but quick and social answer (see chapter 2, "Patterns"). They are looking for us to know them simply and to simply know them.

How do we pose invitations to join small groups? Mostly I've heard from-the-pulpit, generic invitations.

> *An intelligent group . . . does not ask its members to modify their positions in order to let the group reach a decision everyone can be happy with. Instead, it figures out how to use mechanisms—like market prices, or intelligent voting systems—to aggregate and produce collective judgments that represent not what any one person in the group thinks but rather, in some sense, what they all think. Paradoxically, the best way for a group to be smart is for each person in it to think and act as independently as possible.*[4]
>
> —James Surowiecki, *The Wisdom of Crowds*

"Fill out the connection card and someone will contact you."

"There's a group that meets in your neighborhood."

"Stand up, if you're a small group leader. [pause] Okay, everyone. You see who they are. Now pick one of them who looks friendly and look forward to spending time in their homes for the next six weeks. We want everyone to participate."

Is it any wonder we get little more than raised eyebrows?

People want to join as individuals with other individuals. People respond to an invitation that includes people's names instead of an objectified, generic group. "Will you join Bob, Pam, Leslie, Terry, and myself . . ." is a clear invitation for individuals to participate as individuals. The next part of the invitation may be something like, "We would enjoy having you because . . ." Again, clarifying that we want them to participate because of who they are.

Hopefully we've been specific in our "asks" and the people who are on board are there because of their individual gifts. Let's help them live this out!

> *Traditional teams typically operate under the tyranny of the "we"—that is, they put group consensus and constraint above individual freedom. Team harmony is important; conviviality compensates for missing talent. This produces teams with great attitudes and happy members, but, to paraphrase Liebman, "from a polite team comes a polite result."*[5]
> —Bill Fischer and Andy Boynton, "Virtuoso Teams," *Harvard Business Review*

### The Aggregate of Participation Becomes Known

People want their contribution to be part of the contribution of the entire group. They want to know that their individual participation will be accumulated with all the other members' contributions to provide something more robust than they could give by themselves. Is there some organic mechanism—a person or a descriptive system—that turns individuals' thoughts and judgments into a collective thought, decision, or action?

Finding the aggregate is the taking of everyone's stories and using them to build a whole new story—one that makes sense to the whole group. This takes considerable wisdom. It allows groups to move forward.

Finding the aggregate is not the same as reaching consensus. Consensus, when achieved, is little more than taking raw data and totaling it. Consensus, when not reached, translates to frustration and inaction.

## *Remember to Take a Descriptive Approach*

The five elements I have described are not intended to be a prescription for participation. They should not be used as "tricks" to get people to participate. They merely describe environments in which healthy participation naturally emerges.

Sometimes leaders put their faith in master plans because

they have greater faith in master plans than they do in people. Plans are more predictable and easier to control than people. And who controls the plan? Usually one person.

Organic order allows a spirit of diversity, individuality, creativity, and wholeness to emerge. I encourage you to create environments that foster organic participation—environments in which we contribute our individual gifts, and by doing so enrich each other's lives.

# 4

# MEASUREMENT

*recalculating matters*
**moving from bottom line to story**

When Amy came on board as chief financial officer, one of her first assignments was to create a five-year projection. Amy spent about a month evaluating the data. She met with key staff people and gained insight from informal conversations. She studied every report she could gather from suppliers, looking for trends that might signify increases in materials and shipping costs. When the time came for her presentation, Amy felt she was ready.

Amy gathered her portfolio and headed down the hall to Tim's office. She was bubbling with confidence. The data showed a steady pattern of growth, and she looked forward to telling her boss that the company's future looked bright.

Tim, the founder of the company, motioned for Amy to sit at the small conference table next to his desk. "What have you discovered?" he asked as he joined her.

"First, let me give you an overview of the data," she began. "Then we can look at the details."

She handed Tim a single piece of paper, numbers clearly identified and arranged. After he had glanced at the overview, she proceeded with her presentation, handing him a second and a third page. One page charted trends over the previous five years; the next one charted projections for the coming five. She kept her portfolio beside her chair.

"We know what the numbers have been over the past five years. Positive growth. You should feel good about this kind of performance," she said, taking time to let him absorb the information. "My projections for the coming five years also show growth and are somewhat conservative. Actually, I believe we will do better than what I've indicated."

Tim took a few minutes reviewing the report. His face gave no indication of his thoughts.

Finally, Amy broke the silence. "Well, what do you think?"

Tim put the papers down and smiled. "I think you've done well. But how did you come to these conclusions?" Pointing to the graph that showed the projections, Tim stated firmly, "I don't believe this is true."

Amy caught her breath. *Don't let him see you sweat*, she thought. She tried to keep her voice steady.

"The data support these trends," she said, reaching for her portfolio. "I assure you that this analysis is a conservative projection of where we can expect to be in the next five years. In this more detailed report, I can show you how—"

Tim held up his hand to stop her midsentence.

"No," Tim said. "That's fine. I don't need to see everything in that portfolio. As I said, you've done a fine job. Here's my problem," he explained. "You've analyzed the data. You've looked at where we've been, and where you believe we are going. But," he said, referring to a chart, "I know this is wrong."

Amy was shocked. "I don't understand."

"Look at this," Tim said, pointing to the graph [top of opposite page] as he talked. "You have the line starting here and then going upward a bit—smoothly—and upward again as it moves forward."

"Yes," she agreed.

"This is the part I think is wrong. In fact, I think it's not only wrong; it's actually untruthful. Deceptive. A lie."

"A lie?"

"Oh," he reassured her. "I'm not saying *you* are lying. Please

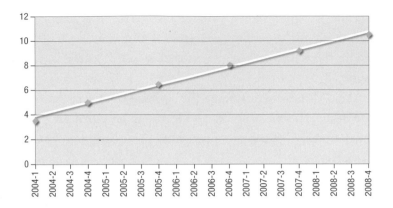

don't take offense. I'm saying that presenting the data this way is erroneous. This graph doesn't tell *enough* of the story to be truthful."

"I still don't follow—" Amy mumbled as her nerves began to settle.

Tim took his pen and drew over Amy's graph:

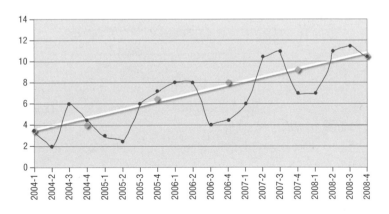

"I suspect that you can foresee months where revenues will probably be down."

"Yes," Amy admitted. "During the startup for the new product line, we will be down. And for years, December has been a 'down' month, even if the year itself is profitable."

"So there are ups and downs that aren't reflected in your graph," Tim asserted.

"Yes. All I did was average the ups and downs to discover the mean. The mean shows an increasing growth trend. The down times . . . yes, they happen, but overall they aren't much to worry about."

"They aren't?" He shook his head. "What happens if I plan using only your chart as a guide? What happens during the 'down' months? I suspect that the raw data will show that in year two, seven of the twelve months will be 'down' months. When those downswings occur, key leaders, employees—everyone— will notice, and they'll start to feel unsettled. If it goes on long enough, panic will set in.

> *"If we only concentrate on the numbers, we'll miss what is really happening."*

"When we go below the trend line, we'll make decisions based on scarcity. When we go above the trend line, we'll make decisions based on surplus."

"I see," Amy responded. "You're saying that if we only concentrate on the numbers, we'll miss what is really happening."

"Exactly," Tim said. "And not just the numbers, but the story behind the numbers. We need to know enough to understand the *whole* story. A chart like the one I've drawn keeps us from focusing too heavily on the end result, upon only one moment in time. In our forecasts, we need to know enough—both highs and lows—to help us with the journey of five years."

## Linear Measurement

Measurement is an important part of our lives. It is a healthy, helpful tool. But many of us have been raised on an unhealthy dose of results-oriented, bottom-line measurement. We develop a program with a mission statement, a vision, values, and goals. We have a clearly defined end. We are certain we know where we are headed and how to get there. We write a proposal that explains the program and informs our supervisors as well as ourselves how we will measure success.

This is the master plan approach to measurement.

Measuring by the bottom line marshals all attention to an end point. The bottom line is an invitation to do whatever is necessary to reach that bottom line. It forces us to think too highly of the highs, and it drives us into panic and depression during the lows.

> *The bottom line is an invitation*
> *to do whatever is necessary*
> *to reach that bottom line.*

Just ask Chris, a recently fired pastor of small groups. Five years ago he was hired to develop small groups in a growing congregation. His program was so successful that he wrote a book about it, a book that was widely read and became a model for other small group leaders.

Last month, Chris lost his job. When we talked about the reasons for this, we discovered that his own standard of measurement became his demise.

"We had a chart," he told me, "which became the reporting tool to evaluate success: number of active groups, number of people meeting per month, number of new groups birthed, how many leaders attended leader meetings, and how many apprentices took the twelve-week training. I even had a manual that defined whether a group was 'active.' We didn't count the 'inactives.'

"The first two years it was great; then we hit a wall. We plateaued. Same number of groups, leaders, apprentices, and so on. This happened four months in a row, then we improved some, but that was it. The numbers weren't down, but they weren't up, either. We were a long way from what I had promised."

"What had you promised?" I wanted to know.

"Everyone in a small group."

"I see."

Chris went on. "I started experimenting with *anything* that had the promise of bringing up the numbers. Some of the ideas worked for a while, and then they didn't. They didn't produce the numbers. Those I reported to started to wonder about my leadership abilities. Frankly, I did too.

"Finally, they let me go. They wanted to find someone who could 'take our small groups program to the next level.'"

So what had happened?

Master plan measurement. Chris, by looking at the bottom line, was actually measuring only part of the truth. There was no mechanism to measure the journey. He hadn't measured how the small group program was answering the question "What are we hoping for?"

In the early development of the program there was a lot of discussion around:

- helping people become connected,
- providing a place where people learned how to live their lives as Christ followers, and

- introducing those not yet following Christ to a community that could help them with their lives.

Though discussed in the beginning, these values didn't find their way to Chris's reporting sheet. Because they were not counted, they lost their importance.

Chris's program was not a failure. Many found their way to Christ. Emails, testimonies, and stories demonstrated that the small group experience had helped many. Chris's leaders shared accounts of their own significant personal change.

Yet, Chris's effectiveness was not measured by the help people received while he was leading. Rather, it was measured by his report of how many people were participating—a bottom-line approach. When the numbers began to stagnate, Chris was deemed to have "failed."

Chris's story illustrates that measurement has these properties:

- We measure that which we perceive to be important.
- That which we measure will become important and will guide our process.
- That which we do not measure will become less important.

Measurement has dynamic power over the journey and the results. It is not neutral. The measurement is the message. Our way of measuring is not a neutral tool that simply tells us what there is to see. No, our way of measuring influences the facts in a way that has a profound effect on our perception of reality. That's why Chris got fired. Measurement, in other words, is serious business.

## Narrative Measurement

Bottom-line, master plan measurement often amounts to numeric, linear, or statistical evaluations. These measurements masquerade as fact but all too often fool us into thinking we're doing better or worse than we really are. If we don't use these tools, how then will we measure success?

Baseball has been asking these questions for years. Baseball is a game of infinite and infinitesimal statistics. Seemingly, almost everything is measured and evaluated. But are the stats on the back of a baseball card the true means of discovering the great players among the good?

For example, a batter lays down a sacrifice bunt to move the runners around the bases. He is successful. The runners are now in scoring position. Yet his stats do not measure this as a positive. The batter who bunted the ball was thrown out at first; it wasn't counted as a hit. But he did the right thing for the team.

*Are the stats on the back of a baseball card the true means of discovering the great players among the good?*

A pitcher can pitch a great game, and have a one-run lead going into the bottom of the ninth inning, when a ball is hit toward left field for a routine out. However, the sun blinds the left fielder and the ball drops in for a double, driving in the man on third and tying the game.

The next batter swings wildly, hoping to distract the catcher and enable the runner to steal third. In this moment of tension, the third baseman misses the catcher's wild throw and the runner comes all the way home.

Do the stats credit the pitcher's great game? No. It's recorded as his loss, even though he had little to do with the poor performance that lost the game.

Or how about the reliever who has a great save record, but in almost every game, he gets into trouble and is repeatedly rescued by the heroic defensive efforts of his fielders. He gets the credit, even though he doesn't pitch that well.

And finally, how about the player who breaks a major-league record but has been accused of using performance-enhancing drugs? Fans and commentators echo the sentiment: "He broke the record, but there will always be an asterisk by his name." The numbers don't tell the truth.[1]

---

*Reducing living organisms to a census count demeans the way we were created.*

---

We must understand what we are measuring. We are talking about measuring life—community, relationships, health. We are not talking about measuring inanimate entities. Reducing living organisms to a census count demeans the way we were created. Even the book of Numbers devotes only about 10 percent of its content to "numbers"; the rest is about the relationship between God and Israel.

John Henry, part-owner of the Boston Red Sox, during a discussion about statistical analysis of baseball, said, "Life is too dynamic to remain static."[2] You bet it is. And life is too dynamic to be measured by the static nature of numbers alone.

> *Life is not measured by the number of breaths we take, but by the number of moments that take our breath away.*
>
> —Author Unknown

Numbers cannot measure life. For example, is quantity of life measured by number of years or experiences? Is a brief life necessarily less full? A long life more so? Or is quantity of life measured against some standard of happiness? If so, how would such a measure be taken?

Last spring, Sara and I added a front porch, new sidewalk, and new driveway to our home. Doing so dramatically increased the value of our property. Our house now has more "curb appeal." The widened driveway makes our cozy home seem larger. The graduated steps now make it easier to navigate the slope of our lawn.

But when we spend an evening on our front porch, do we think about our home's appreciation in dollar value? Do we calculate the return on investment we are likely to realize when the house sells?

No. We measure the value of the porch by the enjoyment we receive when we sit outside and visit with our neighbors. By the evenings we spend reading a book against the backdrop of

> *The quality of our experience is not measured by the seconds on the clock, but by the timelessness of our experience. We fool ourselves if we ask how long it will take before we know who we are, become conscious, identify with our purpose, or remember our own history in a more forgiving way.*
>
> *The things that matter to us are measured by depth. Would you assess your humanity by its pace? When I view myself as a time-sensitive product, valued for what I produce, then I have made depth, extended thought, and the inward journey marginal indulgences.*[3]
>
> —Peter Block, *The Answer to How Is Yes*

children's laughter and dogs barking. By the joy of being part of the story of our neighborhood.

*Story* is the measure of community. Story emerges from life. Ask someone if they had a good day. No matter their response, ask them to elaborate. What you will hear is a story. You will not hear a number. Numbers only arise if they are connected to the story.

## *Story is the universal measurement of life.*

Story is the universal measurement of life.

We know that numbers can be manipulated to say almost anything. We have learned not to trust numbers without context—the story in which a number is situated.

Organic order measures with story. Stories are the measure of the journey. The journey is as important as the end. When thinking through evaluation tools to measure community, story emerges as an effective standard.

But can you develop community with story? Can story be an adequate measuring tool? Can you trust it?

Kennon Callahan has coined a phrase: "persons served in

> It doesn't really matter whether you can quantify your results. What matters is that you rigorously assemble evidence—quantitative or qualitative—to track your progress. If the evidence is primarily qualitative, think like a trial lawyer assembling the combined body of evidence. If the evidence is primarily quantitative, then think of yourself as a laboratory scientist assembling and assessing the data.[4]
>
> —Jim Collins, *Good to Great and the Social Sectors*

mission."[5] He suggests that when we provide our congregational "counts," we remember to count "persons served in mission," not just our members, attendees, and former members. Might I add that by using the words "in mission," Ken is confirming that story is the measurement tool of community. Churches don't become legendary on the community grapevine via reporting of numbers. They become legendary through the sharing of their story of mission within the community.

> Through the mission work of a few people in the congregation, the whole church becomes a legend on the community grapevine. This is a happy by-product of doing mission effectively. The making of a legend doesn't require the participation of everyone in a congregation in that specific mission—after all, there is a diversity of gifts. At the same time, it happens because of the shared, joyful compassion of some doing mission for the sake of mission (not for the sake of becoming a legend).[6]

By collecting these stories, we measure the life—the community—we share.

Vineyard Community Church in Cincinnati practices servant evangelism. On Saturday mornings, teams disperse throughout the city and give out free sodas, clean retail stores' bathrooms, or do whatever other "no strings attached" idea someone has come up with. At lunchtime, the teams regroup back at the church, and over pizza they share the morning's stories.

Shared stories may not fit neat and tidy into a chart or on the back of the Sunday bulletin, but we grow to trust them as a powerful way to measure whether what we are hoping for is taking place. Shared stories are the easiest way to ensure what is important is taken into account. Story helps us measure the life of our communities.

Community cannot exist without story. Stories share and

shape, inform and instruct, motivate and memorialize. Community *is* story.

Stories not only inform how things are going, they connect with the stories of those who are leading and generate wise insights for the future. Stories enable leaders to form a better picture of the health of community than numbers alone ever could.

> *Sound alone is related to present actuality rather than to the past or future. Sound penetrates being. It comes out of the interior of one person and reaches the interior of another person. . . .*
>
> *Where the sounded word is received by the listener there is always community. It takes two to sound! Sound situates us in human community in contrast to later print culture which makes it possible to learn in isolation from other people. . . .*
>
> *[O]ral cultures repeat the traditions of their people many times over. It is only in the telling of the tale that the tradition of the people can be kept alive. The storyteller, therefore, helps to conserve tradition. . . . This story, after all, is the story that legitimizes this community over and against other communities. . . .*
>
> *[M]ost of the storytelling art of Garrison Keillor is precisely episodic and not linear in nature. When I listen to Keillor's stories on the radio or when I read them in his books I do not necessarily listen or read in order to move toward the resolution of the story. Keillor's stories very seldom resolve themselves. It is not because of the ending of the story that we listen and read so intently. We listen and read intently because we enjoy the journey itself.*[7]
>
> —Richard A. Jensen, *Thinking in Story*

# 5

# GROWTH

*progressive evolution*
**moving from bankrupt to sustainable**

I met Marcel at a small groups seminar where I was one of the presenters. Marcel wanted to tell me about his upcoming move. A congregation had asked him to come and establish its first small group program. Marcel had accepted the post under the condition that he be given freedom to experiment. He wanted to develop healthy communities of belonging in the context of that specific congregation. He also wanted time to connect with small group leaders to learn what worked and what didn't. He had already visited with several small group pastors in the community.

Marcel asked me, "What do you know about growing small groups? What do you recommend I try, and what should I stay away from?"

"What have you discovered so far?" I asked.

"I've learned there are many models of growth," Marcel replied. "Most work for some; some don't work for others. Almost all of them seem to have a limited shelf life of success."

Marcel and I had a lengthy conversation that day. During our time together, I shared with him two processes of growth: one that leads to a sustainable, generative whole and another that leads to bankruptcy.

## Large-Lump Growth versus Piecemeal Growth

Christopher Alexander has coined two terms to describe models for growth: *large-lump* and *piecemeal*.

> In large lump development, the environment grows in massive chunks. . . . Once a building is built, it is considered finished; it is not part of a long sequence of repair projects. . . . [It] is based on the fallacy that it is possible to build perfect buildings.[1]

> By piecemeal growth we mean growth that goes forward in small steps, where each project spreads out and adapts itself to the twists and turns of function and site. . . . According to the piecemeal point of view, every environment is changing and growing all the time, in order to keep its use in balance; and the quality of the environment is a kind of semi-stable equilibrium in the flux of time.[2]

Master plan models for implementation of buildings, projects, programs, or other initiatives follow the large-lump approach, which leads to bankruptcy. Organic order models follow the piecemeal approach, which leads to sustainable growth.

The following diagram clarifies the two approaches.

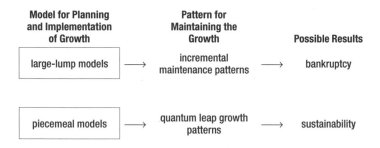

| Model for Planning and Implementation of Growth | | Pattern for Maintaining the Growth | | Possible Results |
|---|---|---|---|---|
| large-lump models | ⟶ | incremental maintenance patterns | ⟶ | bankruptcy |
| piecemeal models | ⟶ | quantum leap growth patterns | ⟶ | sustainability |

At first glance, *piecemeal* and *incremental* seem like synonyms. And in some settings they are. In this discussion, however, *piecemeal* refers to a mindset—the foundational model that you use as you implement the plan. *Incremental* comes about as a result of implementing the plan—it describes the patterns that emerge once the large-lump model is in place.

When you ask the question "How much of the future does

this plan control?" large-lump models would answer with "Most."
Organic order models would answer with "Almost none."

---

## *Organic order models follow the piecemeal approach, which leads to sustainable growth.*

---

Let's illustrate this concept using an example common to
many of us.

Matt and Angie have decided to purchase their first home.
After touring about a dozen of them, they have narrowed their
selections down to two.

Matt is an attorney with a promising future. He is currently
paying his dues, clerking for a municipal judge. Angie is a nurse.
Nurses are in great demand in Matt and Angie's town, and Angie
can command a top salary and generous hours. Matt and Angie
make a good living.

Angie's co-worker, whose husband is also an attorney, recently
moved into a brand-new home in a prestigious subdivision. Matt
and Angie would like to live near this couple, but the prices in
that area are a little steep—at the top of Matt and Angie's price
range. They can afford the purchase but it would be a stretch.

Some of the other homes they looked at were in nice but older
neighborhoods. These homes were not quite as expensive, probably because they did not have the amenities that were so enticing
in the new construction: home office, media room, large master
bedroom with walk-in closet, mudroom, finished basement. But
because the houses are older, maintenance will be a concern.

Which should they choose?

The decision Matt and Angie make will affect their future financial growth. Should they choose the newer home at the top of their price range, they will have to carefully watch what they spend. The bulk of their housing dollar will go toward the mortgage. There will be very little left over to replace the water heater in five years or upgrade the plumbing in twenty.

When these maintenance issues arise, Matt and Angie's budget will be strained, and they may have to reduce the amount of money they direct toward their retirement or college savings plans for the kids.

Should they choose the older home in the median of their price range, they will have some breathing room. When something breaks down in the house, there may be less stress about finding money to make the repair. Their retirement savings will likely not be jeopardized, and Matt and Angie's plans for funding their children's education will probably remain intact.

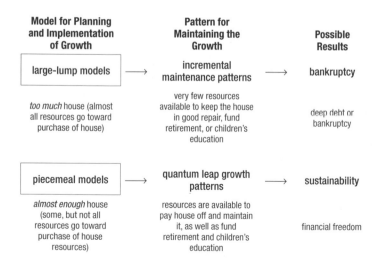

| Model for Planning and Implementation of Growth | | Pattern for Maintaining the Growth | | Possible Results |
|---|---|---|---|---|
| large-lump models | ⟶ | incremental maintenance patterns | ⟶ | bankruptcy |
| *too much* house (almost all resources go toward purchase of house) | | very few resources available to keep the house in good repair, fund retirement, or children's education | | deep debt or bankruptcy |
| piecemeal models | ⟶ | quantum leap growth patterns | ⟶ | sustainability |
| *almost enough* house (some, but not all resources go toward purchase of house resources) | | resources are available to pay house off and maintain it, as well as fund retirement and children's education | | financial freedom |

So what does Matt and Angie's story have to do with large-lump and piecemeal models in churches? Let's visit with George and Mike.

George, senior pastor of a suburban church, attended a seminar on "How to Break the 250 Barrier." The primary solution offered to the attendees was small group ministry. The seminar encouraged each participant to start a small group ministry if they hadn't done so already. And if they had, they were to go home and make it the priority for the coming year.

George was excited about the difference small groups could make in the congregation. This was a way forward that his congregation had not yet tried. He and other key leaders looked aggressively for the best candidate to fill the post of small groups pastor. Mike was hired and he arrived three months after George returned from the seminar. His directive was "make it happen."

Mike's plan was a simple one. Everyone on the membership roll would be placed in a small group according to their age. Mike recruited leaders, divided the congregation into groups of eight to twelve, and required that the groups meet on Wednesday evenings. The whole congregation seemed to be willing and excited to try the new plan for growth.

Before long, obstacles arose. Mike had not anticipated that those who met in the Wednesday night small groups would then limit their involvement in other groups. Even though the other groupings—women's ministries, Bible studies, choir, the church volleyball league—didn't meet on Wednesday nights, ministry leaders began to see a dramatic dip in attendance. Michelle, the youth pastor, complained that key adult sponsors had quit and she couldn't find replacements because people's primary obligation was now to their small groups. The choir lost half its members. George had his hands full with all the complaining about Mike's small group program.

Mike's implementation of a large-lump model for growth had bankrupted other groups, which in turn proved detrimental to the life and mission of the church. The choir had once been strong and provided a warm dynamic to the worship services. The women's groups had kept the needs of missionaries in front of the congregation. Michelle's youth group had provided a home for many of the community's junior and senior high students. And now, these groupings were in jeopardy. Places of connection, care, and growth were starting to die.

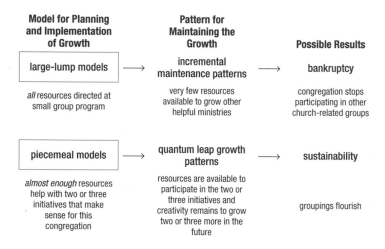

| Model for Planning and Implementation of Growth | Pattern for Maintaining the Growth | Possible Results |
|---|---|---|
| large-lump models $\longrightarrow$ | incremental maintenance patterns $\longrightarrow$ | bankruptcy |
| *all* resources directed at small group program | very few resources available to grow other helpful ministries | congregation stops participating in other church-related groups |
| piecemeal models $\longrightarrow$ | quantum leap growth patterns $\longrightarrow$ | sustainability |
| *almost enough* resources help with two or three initiatives that make sense for this congregation | resources are available to participate in the two or three initiatives and creativity remains to grow two or three more in the future | groupings flourish |

It might have been more helpful if Mike had first gotten to know the parishioners and learned what interested them, not just in church life, but in their whole lives. Had Mike investigated this, he would have learned that small groups already existed throughout the congregation. There was a group of people who had a common interest in dogs. Several individuals regularly went on short-term mission trips. He might have acknowledged that the choir was a significant grouping for people in the congregation.

Had Mike concentrated *some* resources on only two or three

initiatives, he likely would have seen other groupings emerge. Instead, he created his own master plan and expected all to follow. What eventually happened is that people lost interest in both the small groups and their other church groupings, and the whole venture was jeopardized.

## Why Are We Attracted to Large-Lump Models?

So why are we attracted to large-lump models? What benefit do we receive from them?

Our culture has taught us that growth is an expectation. Businesses are expected to deliver double-digit returns every year in order to satisfy shareholders. Individuals are instructed to maximize their potential. Over and over the message is "grow or die."

Choosing a large-lump path toward growth over a piece-meal way forward provides outward evidence of growth sooner. The enormous house, the number of active small groups, the increased attendance in our church services—all demonstrate that growth has occurred. In an odd way, it is a quick fix.

---

*Our culture has taught us that growth is an expectation. . . . Over and over the message is: "Grow or die."*

---

In truth, however, large-lump models rob us of what we are hoping to achieve. One reason this is true is because most—sometimes all—resources are marshaled to build the large-lump plan. Once the large-lump plan is in place, the resources are so depleted that the only possible way to maintain any growth at all is through incremental patterns. The patterns have little momentum, and often bankruptcy results.

In a piecemeal growth pattern, growth may not be evident until later in the process, but the growth is sustainable and leads to a healthy, generative whole. The piecemeal patterns are implemented from the outset, momentum builds, and sustainable growth results.

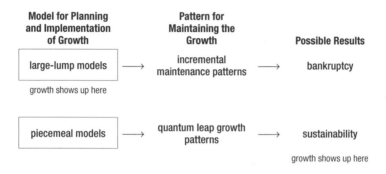

| Model for Planning and Implementation of Growth | | Pattern for Maintaining the Growth | | Possible Results |
|---|---|---|---|---|
| large-lump models | $\longrightarrow$ | incremental maintenance patterns | $\longrightarrow$ | bankruptcy |
| growth shows up here | | | | |
| piecemeal models | $\longrightarrow$ | quantum leap growth patterns | $\longrightarrow$ | sustainability |
| | | | | growth shows up here |

Our company, settingPace, has grown in a piecemeal way. Sara and I began settingPace in our living room. About five years into the venture, we joined forces with another individual. This was a quantum leap forward. Our clients were pleased that we had merged, and they began directing more projects our way. When we realized that we would need to hire employees, we recognized that adding just one employee would not really be helpful. The magnitude of our projects demanded that we add teams of people.

So, our first experience in hiring was the hiring of three people. Our company immediately doubled in size as three went to six. This pattern of hiring in "batches" continued until we had a core group of employees that numbered about sixteen.

Around that time, an opportunity presented itself. A client was closing one of its offices in California. This office was staffed by a wonderful group of people who had worked together for many years. They were experienced and knew our industry well.

*What if we open a West Coast office?* we wondered.

And we did. We did so in a piecemeal way. We did not hire everyone who was being laid off—we hired almost enough people. We did not move them into a brand-new, impressive facility—we instead renovated their existing space to make it fresh and more conducive to our workflow. We did not purchase brand-new furniture—we were able to work out the purchase of their existing furniture with our client, who was happy to help with the new venture.

We had built strong relationships with our clients and a reputation for consistent, quality work. The step of adding a new office propelled us forward in a quantum leap way. This could not have happened had we used a large-lump model to start the office; the piecemeal model made this growth possible.

Jim Collins, in his book *Good to Great* and its accompanying monograph *Good to Great and the Social Sectors*, terms this quantum leap growth as "the flywheel effect."

> In building greatness, there is no single defining action, no grand program, no one killer innovation, no solitary lucky break, no miracle moment. Rather, the process resembles relentlessly pushing a giant, heavy flywheel in one direction, turn upon turn, building momentum until a point of breakthrough, and beyond.[3]

Had we looked at our California office as "grand program, killer innovation, or lucky break" (i.e., as a large-lump solution), we would have been in trouble quickly. We set up the office and within the first month, a publisher dropped the major project the California group was scheduled to complete. We had nine rocky months, but we were able to weather it—barely—because we hadn't bankrupted the entire company to launch the new office.

Consider these questions before you launch your next initiative:

- How much of our future will this *one thing* control?
- Will this *one thing* that I'm planning deplete all or most of our resources?
- Will this *one thing* that I'm planning consume all or most of the community's life?
- If what I'm planning fails, will it devastate the whole?
- If what I'm planning succeeds, will it devastate the whole?

Remember that large-lump growth models bankrupt because they use all resources—present and future. The remaining resources are enough to build momentum only in increments, not in quantum leeps.

Piecemeal growth models don't exhaust the resources available. Instead, they build momentum so quantum leap patterns of growth can emerge.

## *Two Helpful Reminders*

This discussion of growth is not a discussion of big versus small. You can be a small congregation and do a small initiative that bankrupts your congregation. You can be a large congregation and do a small initiative that bankrupts you. It's not about the size of the initiative or the size of the congregation.

Rather, it's about the philosophy behind the initiative. Does this project keep the health of the whole in mind?

A piecemeal model is considerate of the environments into which it plans to introduce growth. A piecemeal model does not consider itself as the "program to end all programs" or a program that provides *the answer.* It proceeds cautiously with the awareness that many existing environments of social vitality are in place. A piecemeal model assumes the purpose of growth is not to overcome these environments but to enhance the current environments with continued health.

> *A piecemeal model is considerate*
> *of the environments into which it plans*
> *to introduce growth.*

Piecemeal models plan on and pay most attention to the opportunities that will catapult growth forward in quantum leaps. Because a piecemeal model is not enamored with itself, it does not look only to its own capacity to sustain growth. A piecemeal model never creates a plan that is so arrogant as to think it is the "only way." Rather, quantum leap growth happens as synergy from all the surrounding environments contributes to the health and growth of the new community. A piecemeal model not only counts on its own energy to grow but mixes its strength with the strengths of surrounding communities to grow forward in quantum leap patterns.

There is a sense of mystery that surrounds growth. I remember going to my great-granddad's farm and listening to his wonderment every spring: "Look! You just plant the seed in the ground and after a few weeks up pops a plant!" he would exclaim. Great-Granddad was always amazed by the growth that he "had no control over."

Great-Granddad viewed growth as something divine, mysterious, and cyclical. Every year he would prepare the field, plant the seed, water and fertilize it. Even so, he trusted the resulting growth was in God's hands.

It is helpful to remember that growth is not something we have total control over. It is also good to know that living things sometimes lie dormant. A seed might appear to be lifeless, but there is in fact an embryo within it, one that is waiting to be activated. Sometimes the activation comes from water and

*Piecemeal growth is the assumption that every environment whether it be for a building, a learning environment or a computer program is continually changing. Piecemeal growth is the opposite of traditional practice, particularly in architecture, which relies on design for replacement. For example a building is created with one purpose in mind. Twenty years later when there are more people it is torn down and replaced with a different building which better suits the current context.*

*Piecemeal growth is an approach which emphasizes design for repair, not replacement. As the environment changes new patterns are selected and applied continually moving the design from one context to another, replacing older designs with more appropriate designs. An example of this is the story about the most beautiful house in the world (Rybczynski 1990). Rybczynski, a professor of architecture, sets out to build a dwelling in which to house the construction of a boat. However, as building proceeds the environment changes and the purpose of the dwelling changes. Eventually, rather than using it to build a boat the structure becomes a place to live. This is an example of piecemeal growth, continually applying patterns to achieve something that you probably would not have predicted in the beginning.[4]*

—David Jones, senior lecturer in information systems,
Central Queensland University

sunlight. Sometimes, as in the case of giant sequoia trees, the activation comes from fire.

Those who advocate large-lump models tend to be afraid of dormant periods. Indeed they should be. Resources are exhausted and there is nothing on which to build the future. It is likely that the venture truly won't have enough energy to "wake up."

---

*Growth is not something we have total control over.*

---

Piecemeal growth has a constant "turning of the flywheel," to use Jim Collins's catchphrase. Even though the venture feels like it's dormant, momentum is building and a quantum pattern will likely emerge.

In the end, "the only Big Plan is to discontinue the Big Plans. The only Big Answer is that there is no Big Answer."[5]

# 6

# POWER

*authority*
**moving from positional to revolving**

The project was running late—months late. Four thousand pages needed to be written and produced by May 15. We were supposed to begin manuscript development in December. Here it was, end of February, and we still had no go-ahead. We knew that the project had not been killed; it still had the May 15 deadline. But our attempts to persuade the client to move the project forward were not producing results.

The client had assigned four individuals to the project. Each person had given us his or her direction as to what we were to do. There were multiple discrepancies among each set of instructions. It was obvious that none of the individuals had shared any information among themselves, even though their cubicles were merely yards apart. Whom should we believe?

We were having a difficult time figuring out who held power over this project. So we looked to the client's organizational chart for assistance. *Surely Jane will make the decision,* we thought.

Well, Jane did make the decision, but none of her four "direct reports" acted on her instruction. Ultimately, we chose a course of action and moved forward with the project. The project was telling us—screaming at us, in fact—to assume power over it. Had we not done so, the project would never have gotten off the ground, much less been completed by its due date.

Master plan tries to deliver power through position. A person is set into a position on an organizational chart and given control, authority, jurisdiction, permission-granting rights, and influence. He or she is trained in how to use these tools to achieve the master plan.

It is an *assumption,* however, that position clearly indicates where power lies. It isn't reality. If power were derived solely from position, why would we need to "learn the ropes"? Learning the ropes is a metaphor for our struggle to figure out the relationships within a group or organization—its formal and informal power structure. We try to discern the "politics" of a situation, mostly out of our need for self-protection and our desire to retain a level of power ourselves.

---

*If power were derived solely from position,*

*why would we need to "learn the ropes"?*

---

If position truly held all power, it would be clear from day one how we should behave, to whom we should listen, and in what channels we should maneuver. We wouldn't need to ask, "What positions hold power?" "What is the organizational path to obtain power?" or "Who is the leader?"

Master plan values the position itself. Organic order values the person more than the position.

Positions have no place of permanent importance with organic order. Rather, organic order sees individuals as people who take on roles. These roles move the project forward and carry a revolving understanding of power. Organic order asks, "Who is *now* the steward of power?" and "Who is *now* leading?"

In a framework of revolving power, there is no dominant member. Like the dynamic game, Rock, Paper, Scissors, no one element stands as permanent leader. Rock smashes Scissors.

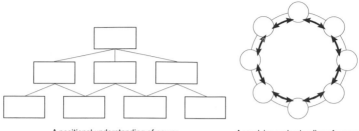

A positional understanding of power          A revolving understanding of power

Scissors cut Paper. Paper covers Rock. This revolving understanding of power gives flow to the game and makes it competitive (and *interesting!*).

Sometimes it is difficult for us to envision what this concept looks like in a business or church setting. So let's examine it in a context with which most of us are very familiar: marriage.

In contemporary Western culture, marriage is generally expected to be a joint, balanced, shared experience. We tend to judge a marriage in which decisions are made solely on the basis of position ("I am the husband" or "I am the wife") to be off-kilter. In fact, we would suspect deep-rooted problems in such a marriage, if not in each partner. We may wonder if abuse exists in the relationship.

We understand that in marriage, certain roles need to be fulfilled. Paying bills, caring for the children, generating income, meeting each partner's sexual needs—all of these "functions" need to be taken care of. We carry out these roles based on who has the competencies and can best fulfill that role at that moment in time.

This spirit of revolving power gives health to the relationship and a solid foundation on which to build the future.

There are three keys to encouraging organic order's spirit of revolving power:

- The project holds the power
- Focus on the whole
- Cross-helping

## *The Project Holds the Power*

One would think that an environment that displays positional power more clearly than almost any other would be that of the armed forces. And it does.

Except when it comes to the reality of the battlefield.

The March 20, 2006, issue of *Newsweek* tells the story of US Navy Lieutenant Commander Richard Jadick, who volunteered to serve as a combat surgeon in Iraq. He accompanied the First Battalion, Eighth Marine Regiment to the city of Fallujah.

He could have performed his role at the base hospital, a relatively safe location forty-five minutes away from the front lines. Instead, on his first day in Iraq, he chose to deploy with a company of soldiers deep into the heart of the urban fighting. By the end of the day—after treating not one but eight soldiers with life-threatening injuries—he knew he wanted to set up an "emergency room in the middle of the battlefield."

The danger was real, the sounds and smells harrowing. But the project—saving lives—was paramount. Positions were not of primary importance.

> Sometimes the corpsmen behaved like the 18- and 19-year-olds they were. Jadick was miffed at one young clerk, in charge of keeping proper records, who had apparently wandered off. Unable to find the man, Jadick began cursing him, when the clerk appeared around the corner. "Where were you?" Jadick angrily demanded. "Well," the clerk said, "some guys were trying to come across through the open gate, so I shot them." Jadick laughed

as he recalled the story. "That's a pretty good excuse, so I'll let you go this time," he told the man.[1]

Technically, the clerk had broken rank; he had left his post. Truthfully, he was honoring an organic order understanding of power. He knew that the project—saving lives—was more important than maintaining the organizational structure of the unit. What good would the positions—the ranks—be if the soldiers they were serving did not even survive to receive treatment?

When the armored ambulances deposited wounded soldiers at the improvised ER, Jadick was not primarily concerned with being "in charge." He was a surgeon first, a lieutenant commander last.

---

*The project—saving lives—was more important than maintaining the organizational structure of the unit.*

---

If Jadick had been a soldier who only understood power in a positional way, he might have been less able to move forward and provide the life-saving help so desperately needed in that battle-scarred building.

Jadick honored an organic order understanding of power. He recognized that insistence on policy and protocol would not have been helpful. Power is not so much a system of submission as it is a system of living that maximizes individual and communal sources of power. Jadick understood the spirit of revolving power—synchronization, improvisation, spontaneity, wisdom, and trust.

Our business serves the educational publishing market. When my wife and I joined forces with another individual, we did so with a mutual understanding that "the project holds the power," although we had not yet coined this phrase. We started our company at a time in our industry when multiple independent parties worked together to create the final product—textbooks. There was a lot of finger-pointing going on among the groups. One party would blame another for negatively affecting their ability to get the job done well or on time.

We promised our clients that this would not happen. Our company would be different.

We recognized that a positional understanding of power was to blame for this struggle. We concluded that power was not something the three of us would possess just because we held the position of "owner." We recognized that each of us would carry different roles and responsibilities, but these roles and responsibilities were not assigned because of position. Rather, they were matched to our strengths. No position anywhere in the company would hold power merely because of the post itself.

As our company has grown, "the project holds the power" has become one of our guiding phrases. When new employees are added, they are amazed at being given power by the project and that we, the owners, don't stand in the way.

## *"The project holds the power."*

Our employees understand that when we take a leadership role within a project, our goal is not to get them to submit to our authority. Rather, we lead because that project "asks" us to do so. The integrity of the project is at stake, not the integrity of our position.

Every project calls for various individuals to play a role in it. Sometimes one role may need to be fulfilled for the entire life of the project. Sometimes a role is very short-lived. Sometimes there is an ebb and flow; the role exists in a fluid state. The point is that the project "tells" us who will steward the power during the many steps between onset and successful completion. The project demands the pacing, the contacts, the leaders, even the steps themselves.

Thus, power is shared in a revolving manner—now you, now Sally, now Ben, now me, back to Sally. We have yet to have a project suggest that only one person hold all the power through the life of the project just because someone holds such-and-such a position.

This one idea has made our company a powerful place. Our success is not dependent upon a "one-positional powerhouse." It is not dependent on a charismatic leader. Everyone within the company participates in the power and shares their sources of power *when called upon by the project*, not because of their position in the company.

Does this mean that we are a "flat" organization, where everyone has the same degree of power at the same time? I'm not sure that a flat organization can truly exist and move forward. A project is always inviting a person to step forward and steward the power. And just as no one person holds positional power, neither do projects hold positional power. Small projects may demand fewer resources than large projects, but all projects are completed with integrity and excellence. Large projects do not attain higher levels of power.

Among people and among projects, the spirit is "revolving," not "flat."

> The Oaks campus has no walls and no secretaries. And
> forget the org chart—the defining unit of operation at
> SEI is the team. Work is distributed among roughly 140
> self-managed teams. Some are permanent, designed to
> serve big customers or important markets. But many are
> temporary: People come together to solve a problem and
> disband when their work is done.
>
> The result is a workplace that's always on the move.
> "We call it fluid leadership," says West. "People figure
> out what they're good at, and that shapes what their
> roles are. There's not just one leader. Different people
> lead during different parts of the process."[2]
>
> —Al West, chairman and CEO, SEI Investments,
> quoted in Scott Kirsner, "Total Teamwork—
> SEI Investments," *Fast Company*

Revolving power is much like a formation of geese flying south. Geese cover long distances with their revolving understanding of power. Various birds take turns leading, cutting through the air and creating a slipstream for the others. If geese flew in a "flat" organization, they would fly in a straight line, increasing fatigue and covering far less distance than that needed for migration.

## *Focus on the Whole*

We joke about "men and their toys." The expensive car in the driveway, the boat docked at the marina, the ATV and the acreage to go with it—all of us could name friends or family members who have made an "excessive purchase." We laugh at this, but underlying our humor is our concern that by purchasing these items, a husband is not thinking about the well-being of his whole family.

Or consider a wife who gets pregnant for the fourth time, even though she knows her husband does not want another child. She has accomplished her goal, but she does not realize the toll this one decision may take on all of her relationships. A fissure develops between the couple and the marriage is jeopardized.

> *A master plan approach . . . is a form of tunnel vision.*

This lack of focus on the whole is characteristic of master plan thinking. The love of positional power typically associated with master plans encourages concentration on what will best serve the position. Organic order, on the other hand, encourages concentration on what will best serve the whole entity, be it a project, relationship, or organization.

A master plan approach often results in what the business literature calls a "silo" system of power. It is a form of tunnel vision. Each person jockeys for positional power in order to command the resources needed to accomplish his or her specific part of the plan. People may be so absorbed by their part of the project that they may lose sight of what the whole project is. They see their role as disconnected from any other—except for those which may help them achieve their goal. They may be unable or unwilling to look beyond their immediate contribution.

Participants concentrate all of their efforts on the success of their particular "silo." They measure success by positional responsibility, not by the success of the whole. When a problem

> *Your structures should be very loose and very flexible: less hierarchy, more opportunity for people to play many different roles. Sometimes you may be a team leader, and at other times you may be a team member. Also, be very flexible with respect to titles, and very fluid in terms of moving people from project to project, depending on the requirements. And be very project oriented, rather than fixed-job oriented.[3]*
> —Rosabeth Moss Kanter, Harvard business professor

arises, so does the comment, "Well, I did my part at least. It's not my fault the thing went wrong."

Revolving power encourages a full view of the whole project so that you know when the project is inviting you to steward the power and when it is asking you to cede power.

Approaching projects in this way is more than "you take this part and I'll take that part." Yes, people can move a project forward by contributing their competencies to a portion of a project. But they do so with the whole clearly in view.

---

*Revolving power brings the security of knowing that you are not the only one the project is relying on.*

---

This view of the whole instills a sense of peace in each participant. They know that the success of the whole is not entirely on their shoulders. When people work in a "silo," they begin to believe that everything depends on them—and them alone. Silos are lonely places. Revolving power brings the security of knowing that you are not the only one the project is relying on.

Peace also comes from knowing that if power is relinquished to someone else, it will return in due time as it revolves through the group. Some people do not relinquish power because they are afraid they will never get it back. Nobody wants to feel powerless. With organic order, not having the power does not equate with powerlessness.

Think of a basketball game. Only one player at any given time can have the ball. Does this mean the other players on the team are not important? Does it mean they are not contributing? Does it mean they have no power?

Absolutely not. In fact, what is happening "away from the ball" is just as important as the point that is being scored or the rebound that is being attempted. What is happening away from the ball is actually helping make the shot or rebound possible.

## Cross-Helping

Pat worked on an assembly line at the local automobile manufacturer. Pat held a particular post along the line and was good at her job.

Her job required precise work in a very tight area. One day the foreman announced that the company was going to institute a system of cross-training. Everyone on the line would learn how to do every job at each post along the line.

This sounded like a great idea. If everyone knew how to do each specific job, then it would make it easier to find someone to fill in when you needed a break, when you were ill and couldn't come in, or when you needed help troubleshooting a problem.

The program was implemented and the people on the line

were cross-trained. The knowledge was instilled; however, the competencies were not. Pat, for example, who was four foot ten and weighed a hundred pounds, was not physically strong enough to fill in for Jeff, no matter how much she cross-trained. And Jeff, whose brawn enabled him to maneuver heavy flats of automobile parts, did not have the small, dexterous fingers that enabled Pat to fulfill her role well.

Before *cross-training*, everyone did their best to help each other in whatever way they could. The workers understood that it wasn't necessary to be an expert at every task. They just needed to bring what skills and knowledge they had and provide help in whatever way they could. I call this *cross-helping*.

The new cross-training program changed this practice. Now people were not permitted to help each other unless they had been cross-trained for that specific job. Instead of it becoming easier for workers to find help, it became harder because "not just anyone" could help. This emphasis on expertise caused pride in some and low morale in others.

Master plan requires that experts provide the help. With organic order, people cross-help. They do not need to be experts to do this. They likely already have some competencies that can nudge a project forward or help a co-worker get caught up. There is no expectation that they will provide all that is needed to accomplish the task.

Cross-*training* is required when position holds the power because you are training for a specific post. When the project holds the power, cross-*helping* is all that is necessary. The project and the people participating in it are highly valued, and people want to help.

Mark was the head chef in a downtown restaurant. Everyone who worked with him was inspired by his love of food, but each day he would come in and complain about having no one willing to help him with the prep work.

"Come on, guys," he would beg. "It isn't hard to do. Man, even a chimp could do it."

---

*Revolving power understands the value*

*of each part that makes the whole.*

*And, it encourages cross-helping*

*as foundational to the whole.*

---

Michelle joined the team. She had come primarily because of Mark's legendary reputation. She looked forward to learning from him.

So she was quite surprised when on their first occasion to work together, he went to the prep table and started his litany against prep work. This puzzled her. Not only was prep her favorite part of the job, she also knew it was critical to the success of any restaurant.

After weeks of listening to his complaints, Michelle spoke up.

"I'll help you, Mark," she offered. "But with one condition," she added. "You must stop putting down the most important part of the job!"

Michelle demonstrated a passion for the task the others had not witnessed before. After a few days they began volunteering to help her with prep. Mark whined, "Why didn't any of you help me?"

Jose replied, "Because you made the job seem insignificant. Michelle has taught us that it is the foundation to a kitchen."

Revolving power understands the value of each part that makes the whole. And, it encourages cross-helping as foundational to the whole.

## Putting the Power Puzzle Together

We've talked a lot about power, but so far we haven't really defined it. I guess I am hesitant to do so because I'm afraid that if we craft a precise definition for power, we will somehow limit our understanding of it.

One thing I do know is that power is more verb than noun (see chapter 9, "Language"). It is action, not object. It is easier to describe how it is used than what it is. It is like love. Something defined more by its expression than by its form.

*Power is more verb than noun.*

Most of us intuitively know what power is. It is more of an essence, less of an entity. Something that is exercised, expressed, enjoyed, and given.

Margaret had been lead soprano in the church choir for ten years. It was an honor given to her by her fellow sopranos after a longtime member retired from the group. Mostly it meant that Margaret organized the music for her section, led the soprano section practice, and called each person to remind them of special needs or to check in if someone was absent. Margaret was the "glue" for the section. She was organizationally competent and fun to be around. She had a spirit of grace and humility.

Margaret was a good singer, although she was not the best

soprano in the group. Not a strong sight-reader, she had learned to follow the flow of the notes well enough to get by. If Margaret needed help with a difficult passage, there were other sopranos who could read music and they would jump in and help.

Margaret loved the choir. It was an important grouping in her life. She particularly loved the practices, during which practices the choir did as much laughing as singing. Margaret always thought that the laughing helped the choir sing with a relaxed spirit of generosity. She likened it to the spirit of *A Prairie Home Companion*—warm and winsome and not too polished.

A few months ago the church hired Mrs. Bassett as the new choir director. She came with high credentials. Everyone was honored that someone of her caliber would come and lead.

The first practice was rocky. Mrs. Bassett didn't find the laughing very productive. She chastised the choir for wasting her time. She replaced "warm and winsome" with *professional* and "not too polished" with *perfect*. And she promised that "no choir of hers" would perform until a piece was flawless. Margaret heard someone say under his breath that this choir would *never* perform if that were the case. Some snickering broke out, and Mrs. Bassett scowled.

By the third practice with Mrs. Bassett, the choir had dwindled to about two-thirds of its original size. Margaret was not having fun anymore. Some of her best friends were no longer finding the time to come to practice.

Mrs. Bassett called a meeting with the section leaders to review their positions and job descriptions. Margaret couldn't remember ever having a "job description."

At the meeting, Mrs. Bassett talked about "asserting leadership authority" and "taking charge of your section." She demanded that the section leaders call each person before every practice to ensure their attendance. And from that point on no one would be allowed to perform if they hadn't made it to every practice. "This will help you motivate them," she said.

Mrs. Bassett distributed a piece of paper that had twenty new policies listed on it. One of them caught Margaret's eye: "Every section leader must know how to read music and conduct the entire choir from time to time."

This was not what Margaret was looking for. She missed her friends. She missed the fun of helping her section try new pieces of music. She missed the spirit of the old choir.

Mrs. Bassett seemed to believe that her position granted her power. Like the conductor of an orchestra, she wanted to influence every aspect of the choir's life. *She* would decide which piece of music would be performed. *She* would recommend how each musical phrase would be interpreted. In short, *she* would make the rules.

Mrs. Bassett sought power but ultimately didn't have it.

In contrast, Margaret had power but didn't seek it. Margaret lived life with an organic order understanding of power. She didn't care about being a section leader. She welcomed everyone's ideas on what songs to sing and what styles of music to try. She was content to let the soprano section have a "starring role" in one piece and a minor role in another. She was happy to share and receive help where needed. She loved the resulting warm spirit that the entire choir shared in practice and the joy she felt in knowing that the performances brought the congregation together as family.

The organic order understanding of power gave Margaret and her fellow musicians the gift of not having to think about power. Because they shared power and did not have a sense of powerlessness, they did not need to look for ways to assert authority. They did not need to try to impose their way of thinking on each other. They were able to act in harmony with each other and with the project. Power emerged within each person.

Isn't this what we hope to invite people to? A place that says: "You and your ideas are welcome. We value you." Top-down approaches are not helpful. The day of organic order has come.

# 7

# COORDINATION

*harmonized energy*
**moving from cooperation to
collaboration**

Think about your day thus far.

You woke up. Did you set an alarm? Why? Do you have to set an alarm every day or did you do so today because you had an early meeting to attend?

What about the kids? Who is picking them up from school? Any soccer games this evening?

You drove to work. Was there traffic? Perhaps you took the subway. Which train did you catch? Was it on time?

You used the photocopier. Did you have to reset it because the previous user's settings didn't match what you needed?

Lunch plans. Meet her *where*? What time?

Upcoming travel. How did you figure that one out, given your responsibilities at work and at home? Somebody will have to help out while you're gone.

Countless times every day, you must solve "coordination problems." You must coordinate your activities and your schedule with other people with whom you share space on this planet. Not just friends and family. Total strangers too. After all, did you recognize every driver on the highway this morning? James Surowiecki has a helpful thought when he states:

> What defines a coordination problem is that to solve it, a person has to think not only about what he believes the right answer is but also about what other people think the right answer is. And that's because what each person does affects and depends on what everyone else will do, and vice versa.[1]

We can solve coordination problems in primarily two ways: via cooperation or via collaboration. Cooperation is the means by which master plan coordinates. Organic order prefers collaboration.

## *Cooperation Wants to Control*

Master plans try to achieve coordination via cooperation. A lot of effort is focused on creating centralized control, consensus, and structural protocols. The kindergarten teacher says to her young charges: "Cooperate with me, children. Cooperate!" The message they receive is: "Do what I say." Government higher-ups issue press releases, calling for individuals to cooperate with this or that investigation. The unspoken statement is: "Don't refuse this request." Sometimes cooperation's themes are: "Don't rock the boat," "It will be easier this way," or "We don't want any conflict here."

The trouble with this is that the spirit of cooperation is a rigid spirit, one that stifles creativity and discovery. It is more concerned with sequence than rhythm. It squashes the human spirit. The master plan becomes the master.

Eric received an email from Jeannette, a supervisor two levels above him. *Wow*, he thought as he read it, *she's asking me to participate on the product development team*. He'd heard about the project, and he was thrilled by the challenge. He wanted to participate.

Scanning the email again, Eric's pulse raced as he read the line ". . . invite your ideas and expertise to move the project forward." He grabbed a sheet of paper and began to scribble notes, jotting down some of the ideas that had come to mind. Over the ensuing days, he spent every free moment thinking about the project, and he began exchanging ideas with other people he knew were on the team.

On the morning when the group assembled for the first time, almost everyone arrived early. The room hummed with energy. Jeannette was last to arrive, accompanied by two assistants, each carrying an armload of three-ring binders.

Jeannette opened the meeting with statements of appreciation, encouragement, and expectation. Then she said, "I've put some thoughts together for us. Jane and Stan are passing out the plan I believe we should follow."

As her helpers handed a binder to each person, she kept talking. "Each of you brings expertise that we need, and I value your cooperation as we work together. Please turn to page one in your binder." Members of the team glanced at each other in bewilderment.

*What happened to collaboration?* Eric wondered. From the looks being exchanged around the table, he was not the only one with this thought. Jeannette's message seemed to be, "Fall into line and help me make this thing work—*please.*"

> *The spirit of cooperation is a rigid spirit,*
> *one that stifles creativity and discovery.*

For Eric, the result was de-motivation. He had anticipated a collaborative experience, but Jeannette was afraid of losing control. Jeannette clearly did not intend to create this dilemma. More likely, she was excited—perhaps a bit daunted—about the project and she took action to advance the group beyond planning to actually doing.

We often make the same mistake. Excited about the possibility of seeing people connect and find a sense of belonging, we create a plan that will most assuredly make it happen. And we fail. People are not primarily looking to cooperate with *our* plan for *their* lives.

Several years ago a congregation began to experience explosive growth in attendance and in mission. A newcomers' class emerged, twelve-week studies where attendees were teamed with a different group and everyone was asked to sit with someone they didn't know. Excitement was high.

---

*People are not primarily looking to cooperate with **our** plan for **their** lives.*

---

Invariably, each class would—on their own—start small groupings in their homes as a way to remain connected. Seeing what was happening, one of the pastors and several key leaders proposed that they hire a small groups coordinator to help the trend continue.

In no time at all, a small groups pastor was brought on board and a master plan for small groups surfaced. Existing groups were required to conform to the plan, to serve as models for new groups.

Study topics were handed down from coordinator to group leader to attendee. Meeting schedules, and in at least one instance, the meeting place, were adjusted to fit the overall design. Mandatory "birthing" would occur when any group passed eleven members.

One year later the number of groups was down by 60 percent. A few months after that, the small groups pastor left for another church.

This church hired a small groups pastor in an effort to gain and maintain control. Yet master plan cooperation gives *control* too significant a role. Cooperation is an effort to control participation. Cooperative control displaces power. Real participative power resides in an environment of spontaneous, oscillating synchronicity, not in an illusion of control.

Denise VanEck, in a sermon titled "The Ache of a Mother," gives a helpful example of the distinction between cooperation and collaboration:

> What was it like for [Eve] as she had that second baby? Did she expect him to be exactly like the first one? What were her assumptions? What were her expectations? What was it like for Eve the first time that she looked at her little boy and thought to herself, "I could give you life, but I can't decide what it is. I can't decide who you are."
>
> I think all of us as moms when we have our babies, we know that they are going to be themselves; they are going to be an individual. But at *some* level we still believe that we can control that person and who they are. I remember the moment for me when I had to learn this lesson.
>
> Steven was [in] about fourth grade, and I had always thought Steve would be my little blonde baseball player—I thought he'd be the little blonde builder like his dad. And so I was always buying him trucks, and trains, and all those boy toys and even though he'd play with them, what he really gravitated toward was the crayons, and the paints, and the clay.
>
> And so by the fourth grade Steve realized that he wanted to be an artist when he grew up, and in order to be an artist he was going to need to study art in Paris. He also realized that he only had about eight more years to get ready.

So he started growing his hair out long, and he bought himself a beret, and then he begged me to spend twenty dollars on "Your First Thousand Words in French."

Steve grows his hair. Pretty soon it's long enough for a ponytail. And this is back in the '80s—this was back when the big movement in the public school systems was the whole self-esteem movement. So I get a call one day from Steve's teacher.

I dutifully go in and the principal is there, and the teacher is there. They say, "Mrs. VanEck, we're very worried about Steve. All the kids tease him about his long hair, his ponytail, and his beret. We think you should get his hair cut."

At that point, I thought there was God and the principal, and if [the principal] told you you had to do something, you had to do it. So I did!

I made an appointment and he went off to get the haircut. I sat in the waiting room and finally I decided I needed to go back there and check on how this was going.

The woman was just finishing this really hideous mullet. [She] turns him around slowly in the chair to face me, and I'm thinking, "Oh, he's going to love his new haircut!" But as she turned him around and I looked at his face, what I saw instead was one tear, dripping down his cheek.

And in that moment everything changed for me as a mom, because that was the moment that I realized that being a mother is more about discovery than it is control. That I had not just gotten my son a really bad haircut—I had violated him. I had violated who he was, I had violated his dreams, I had violated his sense of himself.

And I realized in that moment that I really needed to learn who this little person was. My job wasn't to just buy him baseball caps because that's who I thought that he should be. My job was to make him everything that he could be.[2]

*Just as fireflies and galaxies
and heartbeats and seasons have
organic order, so do we—as beings
created by God.*

When I suggest that people give up on the illusion of control, they sometimes think I am advocating chaos, but this is not the case. I am not saying we should depend on chaos or chance, for there is order in organic order.

I'm saying that just as fireflies and galaxies and heartbeats and seasons have organic order, so do we—as beings created by God.

## Synchronicity Is Collaboration, Not Chaos

Creation is filled with examples of God allowing this spirit of spontaneous synchronicity. My mother moved to Austin, Texas. On our first visit, she took Sara and me to see the Congress Avenue bats. Approximately 750,000 bats live under this highway overpass through the summer months. At dusk, they spontaneously emerge and fly in formation across the sky, searching for food. The noisy mass starts out looking like a giant black cloud. As the bats move off into the distance, their collective form changes and seems like a wisp of smoke, changing with the wind currents. In one sense, the bats move in a chaotic mess. Yet when viewed closer they are moving as a synchronized symphony.

Steven Strogatz describes more examples of nature working in self-organizing ways in his book *Sync: The Emerging Science of*

> *Where did this order come from? Of course it was not planned; there was no master plan. And yet, the regularity, the order, is far too profound to have happened purely by chance. Somehow, the combination of tacit, culture-defined agreements, and traditional approaches to well-known problems, insured that even when people were working separately, they were still working together, sharing the same principles. As a result, no matter how unique and individual the pieces were, there was always an underlying order in the whole.*[3]
>
> —Christopher Alexander and others, *The Oregon Experiment*

*Spontaneous Order.* Strogatz, a professor at Cornell University, has done extensive research on human sleep, circadian rhythms, and other aspects of biological synchronization.

> At the heart of the universe is a steady, insistent beat: the sound of cycles in sync. It pervades nature at every scale from the nucleus to the cosmos. Every night along the tidal rivers of Malaysia, thousands of fireflies congregate in the mangroves and flash in unison, without any leader or cue from the environment. Trillions of electrons march in lockstep in a superconductor, enabling electricity to flow through it with zero resistance. In the solar system, gravitational synchrony can eject huge boulders out of the asteroid belt and toward Earth; the cataclysmic impact of one such meteor is thought to have killed the dinosaurs. Even our bodies are symphonies of rhythm, kept alive by the relentless, coordinated firing of thousands of pacemaker cells in our hearts. In every case, these feats of synchrony occur spontaneously, almost as if nature has an eerie yearning for order.[4]

He continues:

> Scientists have long been baffled by the existence of spontaneous order in the universe. The laws of thermodynamics seem

to dictate the opposite, that nature should inexorably degenerate toward a state of greater disorder, greater entropy. Yet all around us we see magnificent structures—galaxies, cells, ecosystems, human beings—that have somehow managed to assemble themselves.[5]

Collaboration taps into this spirit of synchronicity. Like the organizational tool of growth, collaboration has a generative quality. It generates energy. It generates ideas. It generates power.

Cooperation carries a spirit of force. Power and force are not interchangeable terms. In fact, they are direct opposites.

| Power | Force |
|---|---|
| *Humble* | *Arrogant* |
| *Unassuming* | *Has all the answers* |
| *Supports life* | *Exploits life* |
| *Attracts* | *Repels* |
| *Serves others* | *Self-serving* |
| *Maintains absolute integrity and does not violate principles* | *May violate principles for the sake of expediency* |
| *Relies on truth* | *Relies on rhetoric and propaganda* |
| *Unifies* | *Polarizes* |
| *Appeals to our higher nature* | *Appeals to our lower nature* |

Source: David R. Hawkins, *Power vs. Force: The Hidden Determinants of Human Behavior*, rev. ed. (Carlsbad, CA: Hay House, 2002), 154–56.

Force brings an illusion of control. It does not alleviate chaos. We do need a way for things to work together smoothly, but we could be less concerned with limiting chaos and more interested in achieving a sense of synchronicity. When fostering community, we seek the fluid, graceful movement of birds flying in pattern or a school of fish gliding through deep waters. We are looking for the kind of order that comes from organic, synchronized spontaneity.

# Organic Order Honors Collaboration

Early in our marriage, I applied for an associate pastor position at a nearby church. The congregation was about eighty people strong, and it was serving a growing area of town. The interview time was arranged; Sara and I were to meet the pastor and co-pastor for a get-acquainted dinner at a popular restaurant.

When we arrived, we were surprised to find that the number of interviewers had expanded. The pastor and co-pastor were father and son, and they had brought their wives. We were to be interviewed by the whole family.

We had a pleasant dinner and enjoyed our time together. However, Sara and I learned through the dynamics of the evening that this congregation would be one that desired cooperation, not collaboration.

Contrast this with a congregation in Maine, average attendance sixty-five or so, which Sara's aunt and uncle attend. This congregation has a passion for the children in their community.

During the school year, they hold a once-a-week after-school club. Buses drop the kids off directly from the school, and the kids are welcomed to games, a lesson from the Bible, crafts, and a snack.

In the summertime, the church hosts a morning Vacation Bible School. Kindergartners through fourth graders are invited to this week of fun and Bible lessons.

Both of these endeavors are accomplished with a collaborative spirit, a sense of relaxed intentionality. The congregation knows and participates with the after-school club. The congregation knows and participates with the VBS.

Each time Sara and I have attended this church's Sunday morning worship, we've witnessed a conversation between the attendees (sitting in this early-1800s era New England church building) and their pastor. It's fun to listen to them talk, to hear them share the names of the kids who were helped, and the stories of the helpers.

The conversation is informal and full of grace. There is no talk of "This is how we're going to save Downeast Maine." No "we've got this all figured out. Now this is what we want you to do." In short, no master plan.

Everyone is invited to share the gifts they have. New ideas are welcome. The emphasis is on helping the kids with their lives and doing what will genuinely serve them.

Organic community is not a product, not an end result. Organic community—belonging—is a process, a conversation, a jazz piece, an elegant dance. It is not the *product* of community that we are looking for. It is the *process* of belonging that we long for.

We can help people live out a healthy process of connect-

> *Absurdly, our most important human affairs—marriage, child rearing, education, leadership—do best when there is occasional loss of control and an increase in personal vulnerability, times when we do not know what to do. . . .*
>
> *I used to want to know how to handle my children, my employees, my students, my friends. Now it is a great relief to me to realize that I cannot. Nor, I believe, can anyone else. I especially cannot handle the people I love most. The prospect of such an achievement now appalls me; instead, I think of it as a blessing that I, and we, will never learn.*
>
> *Many of us have the idea that as managers we can use our skills to shape our employees as if we were shaping clay, molding them into what we want them to become. But that isn't the way it really works. It's more as if our employees are piles of clay into which we fall—leaving an impression, all right, and that impression is distinctly us, but it may not be the impression we intended to leave.*[6]
>
> —Richard Farson, *Management of the Absurd*

ing, but not by asking for their cooperation. Do you ask your friends to cooperate with your master plan of friendship? Of course not. Friendship grows out of what you experience together—from connecting, not from falling in line with someone else's program.

---

*Organic community . . . is not the* **product** *of community that we are looking for. It is the* **process** *of belonging that we long for.*

---

Richard Farson, in *Management of the Absurd*, gives another example:

> Think of the difference between seduction and romance. Technique is required for the former but is useless in the latter. Being vulnerable, out of control, buffeted about by the experience, pained at any separation, aching for the next encounter, wild with jealousy, soaring with ecstasy, and plummeting with anxiety—all these are what make it a romance. If you know how to have a romance, it isn't a romance, but a seduction. Not knowing how to do it makes it a romance.[7]

## Collaboration Is a Different Kind of "Intentional"

Master plan cooperation assumes that the more intentional we are, the more likely we are to achieve our goal. But intention may in fact hamper our journey toward organic community.

Often, when people talk about "being intentional," what they mean can be summed up with words such as *purpose-driven, measurable, scientific, deliberate, planned, calculated,* or *premeditated.* The problem is that all of these words are rooted in assumed control, and *community cannot be controlled with intention.*

We can be as intentional with community as we are with going to sleep. It is almost impossible to make yourself go to sleep. In fact, the more intentional you are, the less likely it is that you will fall asleep.

A more helpful way forward is to create an environment in which there is a good chance you will fall asleep. For me this means a cool, dark room; three to four pillows; a frosty cotton sheet layered beneath a warm, heavy blanket; and the songs of Norah Jones playing softly in the background. When these elements are present, I will likely fall asleep. However, there is no guarantee. I have spent many long nights tossing and turning.

The same is true for community. We can have some control over the environments in which community usually emerges, but we have little or no control over community actually emerging. We can intend for the process of community to begin, but we cannot create community intentionally.

Think about the last party you hosted at your home. Did you offer a guarantee to your guests that they would have a good time? That they would make new friends? Of course not.

But I'm sure you did try to create an environment that would help your guests feel comfortable and relaxed. You did your best to include all the elements that would make for a lively social gathering.

You put food out on the table, imagining perhaps that people would linger there, sampling the appetizers and talking with one another.

You probably played some ambient music in the background, soft enough that people wouldn't have to compete with it, but loud enough that it might alleviate awkward pauses in conversation.

You might have grouped chairs together in such a way to facilitate conversation. And so on.

So how can we go about creating such space within the church's life and mission where community can naturally emerge?

First, we must recognize that "space" can take innumerable forms. It certainly includes the physical environment, as mentioned above. Think open spaces, "front porches," coffee kiosks, lobbies with Noah's Ark playground equipment front and center, fresh-baked cookies.

Community can also emerge from creative "space." I know of several churches that encourage artists in the community to exhibit within their facilities. They may propose a theme, or simply invite one individual to display their work. Some congregations have invited local dance troupes and hip-hop groups into their services.

Collaborative space can take the form of a one-time mission event. In 1980 the economy of Poland collapsed. Shortages of food, fuel, and other commodities brought hardship to many.

Jack, a businessman in northeastern Ohio, had contacts with leaders in a small group of Protestant churches in Poland, and he determined to send help. Within weeks a volunteer group had formed, calling themselves "Christians of Encouragement."

Jack had worked as a lobbyist for Senator Hubert H. Humphrey and became the liaison between the group and Washington. Others in the six-member group established relationships with officials in Canada and Poland, spread the word through articles in newspapers and church publications, and appealed to churches and individuals for assistance. A man named Andrzej, in Poland, coordinated the distribution in his country.

"All of us were working over our heads," said Rod, chairman of the group. "Yet God provided. We had to be careful to not get in his way. People we had never heard of called and offered help.

"The six of us met from time to time at the Holiday Inn in Kent, Ohio. Whenever someone saw a need, we didn't say, 'How much will it cost?' but 'How can we get that done?' It was amazing."

Over the course of the next eighteen months, 102 forty-foot shipping containers filled with food, clothing, and medicine were sent from all over the United States and Canada to these churches in Poland. At one point, "Christians of Encouragement" was feeding several thousand babies from five distribution centers in Warsaw.

"When it was over, we packed it in," said Rod. "We never intended to establish an ongoing effort."

Though the project lasted only eighteen months, relationships developed in that project are still strong. The seeds for mission planted in the hearts of congregations here in the US and Canada, and in Poland, continue to bear fruit today.

Neither Jack nor Rod undertook a feasibility study before they began. They did not spend weeks crafting a master plan and trying to fill roles within that plan. People collaborated spontaneously and offered their creativity in a multitude of ways. Their help was richly and generously shared. And they had fun!

The possibilities for creating collaborative space are limitless. And the important thing to recognize is that these possibilities don't have to be orchestrated. Just encouraged. Not discouraged.

> Just as our great cities have bohemian neighborhoods where spontaneity and creativity can thrive, organizations should make room for those aspects of human behavior that authoritarian plans would discourage.[8]
> —Richard Farson, *Management of the Absurd*

A family we know is thinking of finding a new church home. This is significant because they are currently attending the church the wife has attended since she was a child. A new pastor came to serve three years ago and in that time has created an environment of cooperation, not collaboration. His unwillingness to accept anyone's ideas but his own has alienated the congregation. One must wonder why this pastor feels compelled to be in charge of everything.

Are you comfortable in encouraging collaborative spaces where spontaneous organic community can emerge? Will you be able to be at peace with abandoning master plan attempts to control and coordinate?

## A Theological Matter

Our theology influences the way we think about the organizational tool of coordination—more so than any of the other organizational tools. Do we see God as master planner or as creator of organic order?

A theology of God as master planner implies that God has a purpose—even *one* purpose—for your life and it's your lifelong job to pursue it, identify it, and live it out. The gospel becomes, "God has a plan for your life." God has planned *the* job, *the* life partner, *the* house, *the* child, and so on. He wants nothing more than our cooperation with his plan.

A theology of God as creator of organic order, however, allows for collaboration with him. We are privileged to participate with him in the forming of our future. He invites our ideas, our energy, our creativity, our perspective. He gives up a measure of control to facilitate relationship with us and to demonstrate his love.

## *Do we see God as master planner or as creator of organic order?*

In Matthew, Jesus encourages his disciples to understand that their worldview is too limited.

> When Jesus left there, He withdrew to the area of Tyre and Sidon. Just then a Canaanite woman from that region came and kept crying out, "Have mercy on me, Lord, Son of David! My daughter is cruelly tormented by a demon."
>
> Yet He did not say a word to her. So His disciples approached Him and urged Him, "Send her away, because she cries out after us."
>
> He replied, "I was sent only to the lost sheep of the house of Israel."
>
> But she came, knelt before Him, and said, "Lord, help me!"
>
> He answered, "It isn't right to take the children's bread and throw it to their dogs."
>
> "Yes, Lord," she said, "yet even the dogs eat the crumbs that fall from their masters' table!"
>
> Then Jesus replied to her, "Woman, your faith is great. Let it be done for you as you want." And from that moment her daughter was cured.
>
> Matthew 15:21–28

If God can invite collaboration, maybe we can, too.

**131**

# 8

# PARTNERS

*healthy alliances*
**moving from accountability
to edit-ability**

*A*ccountability is the buzzword du jour. The debacles of Enron, WorldCom, Tyco, Adelphia, and so many others have led to an American society obsessed with accountability. These days, any company that develops a master plan of accountability and demonstrates they can keep everyone in line and behaving well will find a receptive hearing among stockholders and stakeholders who nervously seek to protect their investments.

Congress, in an attempt to establish more corporate accountability, passed the Sarbanes-Oxley Act in 2002. Companies large and small are bending under the weight of these well-intentioned regulations. Their operating costs have doubled or tripled as they have added staff and information systems dedicated solely to maintaining compliance with this law.

An accounting system is a way of keeping track. Merriam-Webster Online Dictionary defines *accounting* as "the system of recording and summarizing business and financial transactions and analyzing, verifying, and reporting the results."[1] There are debits and credits, ledgers and registers, principles and regulations. These means of monitoring seem to work well when they are applied to business. But what happens when we apply similar measures to people?

Like the corporate world, the church has had its fair share of scandals. Clergy and parishioners alike are asking for strict measures to assure the sanctity of their faith. Accountability groups are becoming a mainstay for remaining pure.

"Promise Keepers: Men of Integrity" is but one ministry that

133

advocates accountability groups. Millions of men around the world have committed to one another and to their families to abide by the "Seven Promises."[2] Attendees return home from a PK stadium event and form a small group for purposes of fellowship, Bible study, and accountability.

The Promise Keepers website offers some sample accountability questions, which have been culled from various publications. The participant or his accountability partner is to ask such questions as:

- What one sin plagued your walk with God this week?
- Is your thought life pure?
- Did you look at a woman in the wrong way?
- At any time did you compromise your integrity?
- Are you giving to the Lord's work financially?
- Are you walking in total obedience to God?
- Have you lied about any of the previous questions?[3]

Wow! There is such an underlying expectation of failure phrased in a language of absolutes and either/ors. If you truthfully answer any of these questions with a less-than-perfect response, what happens?

"James" was looking for healthy alliances when he joined the "Morning Men" group that met at his church every Thursday at 7:00 a.m. James and his wife, Mariah, were excited about the possibility that James would find some good friends with whom he could "get real." Over the next several weeks James felt accepted by the group. He connected particularly well with Anthony and Bob.

One of the group's stated goals was for each of the men to find an accountability partner or a pair of accountability partners.

The purpose of these relationships was to provide a context in which the men could ask each other "the hard questions." Finally, James found himself awkwardly asking Anthony and Bob if they would become his accountability partners. They accepted with a firm, "Of course!"

To James's surprise, Anthony and Bob came to the first lunch meeting with a list of questions—personal, intimate questions. James was uncomfortable. What was once a wonderful, relaxed friendship now seemed contrived and uneasy. James hesitated to answer the questions, and the responses he did give were ambiguous.

*There is such an underlying expectation of failure phrased in a language of absolutes and either/ors.*

When James talked with Mariah about the experience, they were able to put a finger on why he was so uncomfortable. It seemed like Anthony and Bob were just waiting to catch James in the act of doing something wrong, and that they had taken the responsibility of living his life away from him. But James was looking for help, not another watchdog committee. He had enough of those to deal with at work.

One would hope that most accountability groups are not like James's, but his experience serves to illustrate the point that accountability groups, if gone about in the wrong way, can be awkward and counterproductive.

The AllAboutGOD.com website states that "accountability is essential for any society to function and Christian accountability is no different. We are all held accountable in one way or another. For example, there are laws to obey and if we fail to be obedient, we may have to suffer the consequences set by the officials who hold us accountable. Accountability is simply being responsible for one's actions."[4]

---

*Accountability groups, if gone about in the wrong way, can be awkward and counterproductive.*

---

It would be nice if accountability really was "simply being responsible for one's actions," but in reality, as is implied by the website's analogy with legal codes, accountability often amounts to a relationship whereby *one person holds another person responsible* for his or her actions in a way that is

- *hierarchical*—one person is obedient to another
- *abrasive*—the accountability partner practices "tough love" by being caustic and insensitive
- *unhelpful*—progress toward an integrated life does not happen
- *harmful*—the accountability is psychologically and spiritually damaging

Moreover, the purpose of accountability in many Christian circles is to keep a record of actual behavior versus desired behavior. You may be wondering, "Isn't it a good thing to keep an account of actual behavior versus desired behavior? Doesn't this help us keep our sights on purity and holiness?" Maybe. But

I'm not sure record keeping is the best thing to do if our goal is a relationship that encourages spiritual development. It may be one thing among many things a good friend does, but it should not be the defining element of the relationship. This would go against the spirit of 1 Corinthians 13:5, which says, "Love keeps no record of wrongs" (NIV). Likewise, the psalmist cries out, "If you, O LORD, kept a record of sins, O LORD, who could stand? But with you there is forgiveness" (Psalm 130:3–4 NIV).

It is clear we are searching for partnerships that will nurture

> *Story after story bore this out. The results were invariably tragic. Perhaps the greatest tragedy was that a system promising forgiveness to people and freedom from guilt ended up making so many of them feel guilty.*
>
> *That, in turn, led to chronic legalism. At every turn, they staggered under massive expectations that they never could quite fulfill. Virtually every detail relating to spirituality—Bible reading, prayer, evangelism, church attendance, ministry, missions, financial contributions, even academic studies—was freighted with demands. And failure! They could never do enough. Try as they might, they could never rest in the confidence that God was pleased with them.*
>
> *Thus grace became a theological fiction. Yet rumors of a graceful God persisted. And once people discovered what for so long they had been denied, they felt cheated and outraged and made a beeline for the exit.*
>
> *Overall, the Christianity that my interviewees left had a negative face on it. It often felt like a religion that was constantly trying to get people to believe what they didn't really want to believe, do what they didn't really want to do, and not do what they really did want to do. There was rarely an appeal to the positive. It was as if there was no thought to motivating and helping people do what they genuinely, sincerely, and willfully wanted to do. In fact, efforts at nurturing spiritual growth in ways that felt good and affirming were often dismissed as dangerous.*[5]
>
> —William D. Hendricks, *Exit Interviews*

moral integrity. We know that we cannot do it on our own. We need others to help spur us on. We seek compassionate understanding and wisdom from others who will help us walk the line. Wise help, however, is often hard to come by, and partnering with the wrong person or group of persons can result in devastating shame and disastrous results.

---

*It is clear we are searching for partnerships that will nurture moral integrity.*

---

One such example is related in my previous book, *The Search to Belong*, where I tell the story of a pastor who shares his personal temptations with his Promise Keepers accountability group. His revelations unsettle his "partners," and they eventually force him out of the congregation and the community.

## Edit-ability, Not Accountability

The spirit of organic community is grace, not law; "edit-ability," not accountability. Paul, a close friend of mine, learned the difference between the two approaches in a dramatic way. His first marriage, to an accountant, was an unhappy one. In ways big and small his wife "audited" him. She watched every purchase, she monitored every relationship, she eavesdropped on all phone calls. Every action he took was analyzed and recorded in her mind. She didn't even realize she was doing it. Before long, my friend felt weighted down by his wife's watchfulness and lack of trust. He began to live upward—or, more accurately, downward—to these low expectations.

Paul's second marriage has been much more satisfying. Jane, an editor, lives with a generous spirit of grace. She accepts him and doesn't try to correct or track "errant" behaviors. Instead, she celebrates his gifts and allows him to genuinely celebrate hers. The grace they share with each other is pervasive and contagious.

An editor's function is very different from that of an accountant. While an accountant's training, job, and passion are rooted in looking for errors and covering all bases, an editor's training, job, and passion are to help an author toward richer communication—a rich, full voice that is free of encumbrances. Accountants keep records. Editors wipe away errors while keeping the voice of the author.

An accountant's way to reconcile is through precise conformity to rules; reconciliation comes by way of compliance. Accountants are concerned with reconciling you to a list of desired behaviors. An editor is less concerned with compliance than with communication. Sometimes this means going against rules of grammar, spelling, and punctuation. A good editor wants the author's voice to be the best it can be and thus enforces

> Good editing depends on the exercise of good judgment. For that reason, it is an art, not a science. To be sure, in some aspects of editing—accuracy, grammar, and spelling, for example—there are only right and wrong answers, as often is the case in science. But editing also involves discretion: knowing when to use which word, when to change a word or two for clarity and when to leave a passage as the writer has written it. Often, the best editing decisions are those in which no change is made. Making the right decisions in such cases is clearly an art.[6]
>
> —Floyd K. Baskette, Jack Z. Sissors, and Brian S. Brooks, *The Art of Editing*

rules only when they help the author to be heard. An editor reconciles the author not to rules but to the reader.

---

*Accountants keep records.*
*Editors wipe away errors while keeping*
*the voice of the author.*

---

This is how a good author-editor relationship works: The author submits a rough draft. The editor makes suggestions, even disagrees at times with the author. The author considers the editor's suggestions, and will often make adjustments. The author and editor continue to go back and forth until the project is complete. The entire process is one of give-and-take collaboration.

When presented with the option, most people prefer an author-editor relationship over a client-accountant relationship. We want someone to confide in, pray with, and listen to us. We do not hope for someone to keep a record and reconcile us to the rules. We hope our friends will help us to be reconciled to life, to community, to ourselves, and to God.

> *A light editorial hand is nearly always more effective than a heavy one. An experienced editor will recognize and not tamper with unusual figures of speech and idiomatic usage and will know when to make an editorial change and when simply to suggest it, whether to delete a repetition or an unnecessary recapitulation or simply to point it out to the author, and how to suggest tactfully that an expression may be inappropriate. An author's own style should be respected, whether flamboyant or pedestrian.[7]*
> —*The Chicago Manual of Style*, 15th edition

Alcoholics Anonymous has more the spirit of edit-ability than accountability. Yes, it has "Twelve Steps," but these steps are a descriptive pattern for sobriety (see chapter 2, "Patterns"). They describe a healthy life. There are no bullet points or subheads that list how each step should be lived out.[8]

Accountability groups tend to set up rules and conditions for you to live by. Your accountability partner's job is to make sure you're following the master plan. That is not the case in an AA group. Your sponsor listens to you, coaches you, and deals with you truthfully; however, he or she does not assume your problems. He or she does not "work the steps" for you. The problem stays with you.

*When presented with the option, most people prefer an author-editor relationship over a client-accountant relationship.*

The wisdom of AA (and similar groups that have the spirit of edit-ability) is that it lives out and honors the descriptive nature of the Twelve Steps. The downfall of unhealthy accountability groups is that they take a descriptive list, such as the Twelve Steps or Seven Promises, and create from it a prescriptive set of expectations.

It's important to remember that a manuscript does not come to an editor in perfect shape. Likewise, no individual comes to a given community in perfect shape. So using language of perfection is unwise and counterproductive.

The following chart explains some of the differences between accountability relationships and edit-ability relationships.

| Accountability Relationships | Edit-ability Relationships |
| --- | --- |
| • *Accountability relationships are built on the understanding that people are primarily bad and sinful.* | • *Edit-ability relationships are built on the understanding that people are good, made in the image of God.* |
| • *The accountability partner looks for mistakes and keeps an account.* | • *The editor looks for strengths and makes suggestions for improvement.* |
| • *The accountability partner initiates accountability discussions on a regular schedule or on whatever schedule the accountability partner deems necessary for proper recording.* | • *In a relationship of edit-ability, one person brings requests for help to the other on an as-needed basis.* |
| • *The accountability partner tries to help by creating more structure, rules, and regulations.* | • *The editor makes suggestions but leaves the major reworking with the individual.* |
| • *The accountability partner is often drawn from a limited resource pool (e.g., someone within the individual's organized small group).* | • *The editor is a person of one's own choosing, in whatever sphere of life would be helpful.* |
| • *The accountability partner tries to get the individual to cooperate with and conform to certain standards and expectations (a prescriptive pattern).* | • *The editor allows one to resource oneself in whatever ways are healthy (a descriptive pattern). The relationship is more about collaboration than cooperation.* |
| • *The accountability partner emphasizes and inadvertently reinforces the negative behavior by concentrating on it.* | • *In an edit-ability relationship, the people involved celebrate the journey of wholeness.* |
| • *The accountability partner holds the power.* | • *The project—health or wholeness— holds the power.* |

Galatians 6:1–2 says: "Brothers, if someone is caught in any wrongdoing, you who are spiritual should restore such a person with a gentle spirit, watching out for yourselves so you won't be tempted also. Carry one another's burdens; in this way you will fulfill the law of Christ." Sometimes, we justify our master plan of accountability by emphasizing the second verse. However, the spirit of verse 1 is twofold: someone is *caught* in wrongdoing (the behavior was not looked for) and we are to watch out for ourselves that the same thing doesn't happen to us. The "problems" of living are left as our own responsibility, which is the reminder given to us in verse 5: "For each person will have to carry his own load."

> *As sponsors, we are to share our experience, strength, and hope with our sponsees rather than tell them what to do. Even the Twelve Steps are "suggested." Sponsees deserve to make the basic decisions about their lives including whether or not to work their program or to stay in recovery. As their sponsors, we are entitled to suggest, but not to dictate. One of our responsibilities is to prepare our sponsees to be accountable and responsible for their own behavior. We can't accomplish that objective if we are telling them what to do. They have a right to their own mistakes and to the lessons they will learn from them.*[9]
>
> —Hamilton B. *Twelve Step Sponsorship*

It's not about catching someone. It's not about keeping track. It's not about laws. It's about finding health—the health that grace and a gentle spirit can bring about, through the compassion of Christ.

# 9

# LANGUAGE

*future lingo*
**moving from noun-centric
to verb-centric**

**Y**ou may find this chapter to be a stretch. This chapter describes the genesis of an idea. A way of thinking about language that may fall outside your comfort zone. Hang in there and think with me on this one.

Part of the problem is this: we can only talk about—and think about—language by using language. Were we able to pick up *language*, carry it into the lab, measure it, weigh it, photograph it, handle it, and otherwise treat it as a *thing*, our problem would diminish.

But we can't. Were we able to do so, we would be in the midst of the dilemma that I will try to steer us away from in this chapter.

Let's proceed nonetheless.

This book is about ways to develop organic community using the nine organizational tools in an organic order way rather than in a master plan way. You may have noticed that we often made distinctions between individual words.

This is intentional. There *is* a difference between *collaboration* and *cooperation*. There *is* a difference between *bankrupt* and *sustainable*. The words that we choose reflect what is in our heart.

Language matters. Words matter.

It may help to keep in mind what words are. Words are symbols for what we are trying to communicate.

For example, when we say *tree*, the word itself (T-R-E-E) is not what we are communicating. Rather we are wanting to convey the *idea* of a tree. *Tree* is only a symbol that draws in each of our minds an image of a tree. It may be a real tree or an imaginary tree, such as one in a sketch or a painting. Unless you and I are looking at the same tree at the same time and from the same perspective, your image of *tree* and my image of *tree* are probably different.

Both of us know this, yet each of us recognizes what we mean by the word. Our mental pictures of *tree* are similar enough that we know what the other means by the word *tree*.

Thus, words are symbols. Metaphors. And as we discuss words, specifically the words *noun* and *verb*, it will be helpful to remember that we are not talking about the words themselves. In this chapter we are talking about what *noun* and *verb* mean metaphorically.

Here's another factor to remember: language is living. Today's English is anything but a dead language.

Here's an example: For centuries the word *icon* meant "sacred painting." Need I mention today's more common meaning?

Prior to the development of a certain type of engine, the word *jet* as a verb meant "to spout forth" or "to emit in a stream," or as a noun a particular shade of black (Webster's).

When I was in junior high, the word *bad* actually meant something that was good in the extreme, similar to the way today's young people use the expression, "Shut up!" or "That's ridiculous!" It's meant as a compliment!

*Apple* does not only mean a pomaceous fruit, nor *Blackberry* a specific bramble.

Plus, new words constantly come into play: *euro* (money); *moped* (the motorbike, not the pouting); *crawl* (not the action on the floor but the action on the bottom of the screen); and on and on.

Words formerly considered nouns may emerge as verbs.

Webster's online unabridged dictionary lists *impact* as a noun, defined as "a forceful contact, collision, or onset." Today, *impact* also means "to have an effect on."

Nonnative English speakers and immigrants in particular must go *nuts* (another word with more than one meaning) trying to figure out our language. Yet people within their own cultures are able to make these kinds of word-meaning transitions fairly easily, because only a few words are changing at any given time. To change the meaning of the word *jet*, for example, took half a generation. Acceptance of the new meaning for *icon* took only a few months.

## A More Fundamental Shift

We are changing not only the meanings of some of our words but also the very structure of how we form our sentences. Our understanding of this fundamental shift will affect how—perhaps even whether—we are able to connect future generations with the gospel.

*We live in a noun-centric culture.*

As English-speaking people, we live in a noun-centric culture. In any sentence, the noun (or pronoun) is the most important word or idea. The rest of the sentence supports the noun.

Thus, for something to be important, and to make it possible for us to talk about that important item, we must make it a noun.

So we become noun architects.

This is beginning to change, however. We are moving from a

noun-centric to a more verb-centric language, meaning that the verb is becoming the main idea of the sentence. Some indications of these changes, and the influences behind them, are

- word clustering
- Internet influences
- acceptance of quantum theory
- open source code initiatives

Increasingly, we are using several words to describe one thing being experienced. One word (a noun) is no longer sufficient. I hear people cluster words like *community, belonging, cell groups,* and *small groups* in the same sentence, as synonyms. They do so because they cannot find one word (a noun) to describe the whole experience they want to convey. They instinctively know that by assigning only one word, they are creating something static and limited.

Rather than create a static entity using only one noun, they instead cluster several nouns as a means of making the nouns dynamic—more verblike. They want to describe the process, the experience, the "being" in community.

The poet has struggled with this puzzle for a long time. Attempting to describe love, art, and music in a single word leaves you feeling incomplete or hollow. But this is no longer a puzzle only for the poets; it has seeped into our everyday lives. Word-clustering is a way we express the verb-centric world in which we live and play. We will see this more and more as we move toward more verb-centric language.

The English language has many nouns that are impossible to disconnect from the idea of relationship, such as love, scorn, or friendship. Words like *telephone, radio, system, railroad, canal, organization, nation, culture,* even words such as *moon, child, neighbor, supervisor* (all nouns), have a relational connotation and cannot be understood apart from that relational connotation. We see them as more verblike (dynamic) than nounlike (static).

For example, the moon cannot be fully understood without knowing its relationship to the sun and earth. Through knowing the relationship, we gain better understanding of our whole world. Many times when we are talking about the moon, we are not talking about the object in the sky. Rather, we are talking about its dominance in our lives—the comfort we receive from its presence every evening, the regularity of the tides, the romance that seeps into the air on a softly lit night.

The Internet has started to clear the way for us to begin to accept and experiment with shifting away from a noun-centered to a more verb-centric lexicon. Almost all Internet language describes relational activity. *Blog, RSS, email, Wikipedia, Google,* and *eBay* are all relational verbs, so to speak.

The Internet has produced a newer, more action-oriented, verb-dominated language. It has made the globe smaller and has allowed mystery to reemerge.

*Almost all Internet language describes relational activity.*

It has made the world relationally more accessible. This closeness has produced a mingling of ideas, knowledge, and language. So when our noun-centric culture mingles with a verb-centric culture, our language changes and keeps changing. This mingling is like two DNA strains merging to generate an entirely different yet similar DNA code.

Hand in hand with widespread use of the Internet is the reemergence of mystery without the pervasive need to solve it. A noun-centric culture tends to deny and suppress mystery. Mystery is more welcome in verb-centric thinking.

In a noun-centric setting, if mystery does raise its head, someone will attach a noun descriptor to put mystery in its place. We tend to feel that if there is a noun (name) for something, then—because it is now known—it is no longer a mystery. Mystery is best described in verb.

Moving to quantum theory, here we encounter thought written in verbs. The theory of *quantum entanglement,* for example, supports the idea that everything is entangled in a relational web with everything. Particles of energy/matter can become correlated with other particles of energy/matter and will relate to each other even over distance. No object stands alone as a singular object.

Everything is in a relational verb. Even the act of standing alone is a relational verb whereby everything else is affected. *Entangled in action*—all matter acts as a verb and nothing stands alone as a noun.

The widespread acceptance of these views on entanglement and other staples of quantum theory are having a widespread acceptance on the language that can be used to discuss experience.

Finally, computer programming languages are transitioning from closed, proprietary systems to open source code. Closed languages are under the control of the developers. Programmers logically think through the desired outputs and program routines into the code to achieve these outputs. The code is static—nounlike. Only the company-authorized programmers can change the code.

Open source code, however, is more dynamic in its nature.

Although programmers still write code, the developer publishes the base code and makes it available to everyone. Anyone who is interested in modifying the code can do so. There are no restrictions placed on it. One person might modify the code to be applicable in the field of genetics. Another might modify the code to fit his environment of graphic design. These modifications are then made available to everyone. And so the code lives. In a very real sense, the code becomes a verb, a dynamic connection between users, a very real community.

Because of these indicators, it may be helpful to start recognizing that many things we describe as nouns are really more verblike. Let's explore several examples.

*Fire.*

Fire is not an object. It isn't a person, place, or thing. Fire is an ongoing process. It has no substance. However, when we talk about fire we must objectify it and make it a noun so that we can structure a sentence around it. Much the same could be said of words such as *explosion, breath, flight,* and so on.

*Love.* Is love an object? Can you weigh love? Photograph love? Measure love in inches? Love is relational. Love can be understood best as a verb.

*Music.*

*Art.*

*Home.*

You get the point. But does the concept go further? What about words like *person? Person* may be a noun, but is that all person is? How do you like it when someone treats you only as "person, place, or thing"? As primarily noun? I doubt my wife would like to be described in a single word!

What about sacred words such as *church, congregation, worship, God?* If we were to see these equally as verbs as well as nouns, how would that influence our theology? Our infatuation with nouns may have led us to describe the Holy in terms of a noun's need to objectify, limit, even control.

We are hesitant to express the Holy as verb and then operate accordingly. God is easier to get our minds, concepts, and theology around if the Godhead remains only noun.

Nouns provide certainty. Identity. Position. Stability. Nouns supply the answer to "What?" They describe a finite solution and thus are the central language of master plan.

Nouns minimize relational action. Nouns rein in verbs' constant movement, constant activity. How can we observe, test, or dissect something if it doesn't hold still for us?

To say that nouns are "person, place, or thing" gives only a partial snapshot and may not give the solution we need. It is like taking the measurement of a person at a given point in time, without "story." Verbs tell the story. For life's complex and confusing conundrums, we need verbs, not nouns.

Verbs describe an ongoing process. Human beings, for example, become. We are constantly in motion; constantly changing; we are not still and unmoving. A snapshot of a person is not who they are; it is only a representation of a minute part of what they may be at a specific moment.

Plus, we are in a constant state of *relating*. However, when viewed as an objective noun we are treated as inanimate—without personality, individuality, and growth.

Nouns may be neat, may be hygienic, but also may fail to deliver. To maximize only the noun and minimize the verb leads us to develop static and absolute structures, structures that might promise help and health, yet provide a sterile and unhelpful understanding of what life is really about.

God describes himself with the verb "I am." The Trinity is not three objects. The Trinity is a dance of three verbs. Three "I ams."

How would it affect our theology if we emphasized God-verb in the same ways we have traditionally emphasized God-noun? Even more, God-verb relating with man-verb? Of God as moving, acting, doing, rather than God as sitting, motionless, static—relating to the changes and actions of mankind?

---

*Verbs describe an ongoing process.*
*Human beings, for example, become.*

---

This might narrow the gap between the evolutionist and his view of changes in the natural world on the one hand and the view that life on earth has remained static and unchanging on the other.

Or maybe we would no longer treat God, Jesus, and the Spirit as separate beings, and thus could give a little clearer explanation of the three-in-one concept.

And maybe we would stop expecting God, or the words written about him (the Bible), to be "the answer." God as noun can become *answer*. God as verb can become a *relational experience*.

Phrases like "objective truth" and "absolute truth" are comfortable in a noun-centric culture and language. They are less comfortable in a verb-centric culture, perhaps because we who are ever-changing recognize that our understanding is ever-changing as well.

A noun-centric view interprets "I am the way, the truth, and the life" differently from a verb-centric view. In the noun-centric world, Jesus expresses an objectified, absolute statement. If you were to look for "it" long enough, you would find "it" in way, truth, and life. In a verb-centric world, Jesus is expressing relational characteristics experienced as you and he together explore way, truth, and life. In the latter view, way, truth, and life are continuing, ongoing; not final, not concluded.

## From Noun-Centric to Verb-Centric

What if we elevated verb? What if we metaphorically moved to a verb-centric world rather than a noun-centric world, where the verb housed the central idea? What difference would that make?

This last year I went through a dramatic change in life stage: my daughter turned eighteen. And even though I know it didn't happen overnight, it seemed that overnight she had changed from needing my guidance to preferring her own way. She is now deciding things I once had some influence and control over. Though I never have felt like I objectified her as *child*, I now realize in a clearer and richer way she is not merely *noun*. She is definitely *verb*. I sometimes wish she were *noun* so I could gain some control again, yet I want her to always remains *verb*.

So what? What difference does it make—noun-centric or verb-centric? The difference is this: Language not only expresses

> *Human beings do not live in the objective world alone, nor alone in the world of social activity as ordinarily understood, but are very much at the mercy of the particular language which has become the medium of expression for their society. . . . The fact of the matter is that the "real world" is to a large extent unconsciously built upon the language habits of the group. No two languages are ever sufficiently similar to be considered as representing the same social reality. The worlds in which different societies live are distinct worlds, not merely the same world with different labels attached.[1]*
>
> —Zdenek Salzmann, *Language, Culture and Society*

social structures. Language also shapes worldview. Language shapes the way we behave and believe.

Do you view community, belonging, and small groups as nouns or verbs? This is more than an interesting question to wrestle with. Whether you view these as noun or verb will affect your language, your processes, your structures, and yes, even your outcomes.

---

## *Language shapes the way we behave and believe.*

---

For example, *small group* viewed as noun allows us to treat it as an object that we can control at some level. This view gives us permission to think that if we could come up with *the one way* of structuring a small groups program, then everyone would want to be involved.

*One way* would be *the way*—for everyone.

This may lead us to say things like, "Everyone needs to participate in one of our church-sponsored small groups if you want to grow and belong." This silver bullet approach not only objectifies the group but every individual in the group. Everyone, and every group, becomes a widget that we can mold, maneuver, organize, direct, and yes—control.

Soon participants begin thinking, *I beg your pardon; I'm not a widget!* They are begging to be treated as living and organic—as *verb*. People as well as groups (which we should always remind ourselves are made up of individuals) want to be treated in an organic way, not in a sterile, inorganic way.

Whether or not our English language moves farther toward emphasizing verb rather than noun, our group life will benefit

**155**

as we move in this direction ourselves. Can you become verb-centric, rather than noun-centric?

The next time you hear a new method for developing community, small groups, cell groups, or whatever; or as you develop the next structure for your congregation; or the next time you prepare to preach, or the next time you lead worship, ask yourself: "What am I treating as *noun* that is really *verb*?"

As you've learned, the nine organizational tools can be viewed in a master plan way or in an organic order way. Master plan looks at these tools as nouns. Organic order sees these tools as verbs.

Master plan must hold on to the noun in order to service "the plan."

Organic order is open sourced, less concerned with holding on, more intent with going forward in the messy, relational,

---

*Ask yourself: "What am I treating*
*as **noun** that really is **verb**?"*

---

living verb of who we are, who God is, and what our life and the lives of those we serve is indeed about.

During the 2004 presidential election, candidate Howard Dean was extolled as an example of someone who took advantage of all the tools that were available to him. He was one of the first politicians to recognize the power of the Internet in a campaign.

Whether he intended to do so or not, he heralded in a new era of "open-source politics." Jonathan Alter of *Newsweek* describes some of the implications this will have on future elections:

Open-source politics has its hazards, starting with the fact that most people over 35 will need some help with the concept. But just as Linux lets tech-savvy users avoid Microsoft and design their own operating systems, so "netroots" political organizers may succeed in redesigning our current nominating system. But there probably won't be much that's organized about it. By definition, the Internet strips big shots of their control of the process, which is a good thing. Politics is at its most invigorating when it's cacophonous and chaotic.[2]

Unlike Mr. Alter, I do believe there is order within organic order. I don't believe there is total chaos within open-source environments. Check out www.opensource.org and you'll see how much order there actually is within the open-source movement.

Programmers of old were master planners. They wrote the code, and you had to live within the code. Remember how you felt when you came up against something in a program that you could not get around? You felt limited, powerless.

Those in our church "programs" may feel the same. They may feel like nouns, very static and still. With organic order, we have an opportunity to be open sources of help and hope, open sources of creativity, of imagination, of grace.

Don't be afraid to let your language change and evolve to reflect the world around you. Our language is as dynamic as our relationships are. Enjoy the movement!

# 10 RESOURCES

*mining wherewithal*
**moving from scarcity to abundancy**

**M**ost of us have members of the family who become symbols—caricatures in family folklore. Mine is no exception. I've heard many anecdotes that have helped me understand the origins of my family's attitudes, values, and spirit.

Many stories revolve around my grandparents' attitudes toward money. As I remember it, my grandparents lived in a nice home in a nice neighborhood. Grandma kept the house and Grandpa worked as the head of engineering production in a local glass factory. They lived comfortably modest lives.

They had very different views on finances. Grandpa worried little, if at all, about how much money was needed for tomorrow. He was confident that he had the capacity to develop whatever resources were needed for the future. At worst, his view was "Spend today, for tomorrow may never come." At best, Grandpa lived with a spirit of adventure, grace, and generosity.

Grandma, on the other hand, worried about their financial future much of the time. She "knew" there would never be enough. When her worry was excessive, she seemed stingy, tight, and grumpy. When her fears were at a minimum, she would laugh and say, "We're saving for a rainy day."

It was impossible for her to live life with a spirit of abundancy (more on this term in a bit). She and Grandpa didn't have an abundance, and it didn't seem likely that they ever would. She saw the weekly checks. They were all the same. She saw the monthly bills and they were all they same—sometimes more. Nothing would change. Abundance was impossible.

Grandma also thought it was improper to tackle life with what was—to her way of thinking—such a flippant, immature, and irresponsible attitude. She remembered the Depression. An attitude of abundance was akin to an attitude of waste. And waste was unwise and ungodly.

Keith Johnstone says, "There are people who prefer to say 'Yes,' and there are people who would prefer to say 'No.' Those who say 'Yes' are rewarded by the adventures they have, and those who say 'No' are rewarded by the safety they attain."[1]

My grandma preferred "No."

For whatever reason, she longed for safety. So she nurtured a spirit of scarcity. She equated Grandpa's spirit of abundancy to real and present danger. The adventures of living with this spirit turned her stomach.

## *Too Quick to Ask "How?"*

Master plans begin with the question "Where are we headed?" followed immediately by "How are we going to get there?" These become the central questions. They are intended to secure safety, but really they result in a plan that prescribes the "how" prematurely.

Master plan believes that all questions will be resolved by

*In any of its hundreds of variations when we ask How? we are really making a statement: What we lack is the right tool. The right methodology. We are mechanics who cannot find the right wrench. The question How? not only expresses doubt about whether we know enough and are enough; it also affirms the belief that what works is the defining question, a major source of our identity.*[2]

—Peter Block, *The Answer to How Is Yes*

going through the process of asking and answering "How?" But many times the question "How?" isn't a question at all. Rather, it is a comment rooted in a spirit of scarcity. A quick "How?" confirms that we are not enough and that we don't have enough. It reveals that we may live with a spirit of scarcity.

Scarcity is a worldview; it is not necessarily truth. I've known people who have more than enough, yet they live with a worldview of scarcity. I've also known people who don't have enough, yet they live with a spirit of abundancy. We've all seen stingy wealthy persons and generous poor persons. The spirit of scarcity is a personal view of the resources available.

*Scarcity is a worldview; it is not necessarily truth.*

My grandpa lived with a spirit of abundancy. This too is a view and may not be reality. Grandpa believed there was always enough and there would always be enough. His spirit of abundancy opened the door for spontaneity, adventure, synchronicity, and the generosity of possibility.

This spirit served him well. One of the oft-repeated family legends is that one day, Grandpa's boss and other members of the engineering team presented him with a problem that needed his expertise. He was asked to design a glass machine that would provide a solution to a specific problem. As he studied the data, he was unaware that the problem he was trying to solve was fictitious and mathematically impossible. His boss and team members were trying to pull a fast one on him.

At the end of a couple days' work, Grandpa presented his boss with a possible solution. His boss and co-workers looked over the drawings in disbelief. Ultimately, the machine was assembled and is still blowing formed glass bottles.

My grandpa almost always skipped the "How?" question and went straight to the possible solutions. It's not so much that he didn't *answer* "How?"—it's that he didn't really *ask* the question. His spirit was more "This can be accomplished by . . ." and not "How can we ever accomplish this?"

When we make "How?" a comment, we reveal that we may live with a spirit of scarcity. Those who skip asking the question and head straight to the possibilities probably live with a spirit of abundancy.

## Abundance, Abundant, and Abundancy

*Abundancy* is the word I'm using to describe the spirit of this worldview. As I mentioned, the spirit of abundancy may not describe reality. It is not necessarily true that a person who lives with a spirit of abundancy *has* an abundance. Nor am I promoting that people have a spirit of *abundance. Abundance* communicates "more than enough."

> *The spirit of abundancy is a celebration*
> *of possibilities.*

People do not need an abundance to operate in an organic order way. Nor do they need to think they have everything in place to resource organic order. Abundancy doesn't mean complete or limitless.

The spirit of abundancy is a celebration of possibilities. Abundancy knows there are many possibilities—some that are well in place, some that are known, and some that are yet to be discovered. It finds comfort in the number of possibilities; having so many secures robustness.

Monica, the small groups coordinator of her congregation and the mother of an eleven-year-old soccer player, noticed that the families of her son's team lingered after the Saturday afternoon soccer practices. The kids gathered together and kicked soccer balls around while they waited for their parents to finish talking. This happened with such regularity that Monica realized the families had formed an informal small group.

Monica thought this after-practice small group idea could work in other settings. She didn't know exactly how the idea could be developed, but she knew that Bill, a legendary community soccer coach, had a passion for people and their search to connect. He would likely have fun with the idea.

Monica presented the idea to her elder board, knowing that additional funds would be needed and she would have to secure their approval before she could move forward. The elders listened enthusiastically and approved the idea with one condition—that one of the men in the congregation lead the venture, not Bill. Bill, after all, didn't attend their church.

The elders were operating under a mindset of scarcity. The only resources they saw as available to them were those within their congregation. The thought of allowing Bill to lead in this way left them feeling insecure. The elders lessened the potential for success in order to increase their level of perceived safety.

One other distinction we should make is that between the words *possibility* and *option*. *Option* implies that once we choose one, we must follow it to completion. The word *possibility* has an open-ended spirit. It is more like a brainstorming session than a decision tree. Organic order's spirit of abundancy celebrates the abundance of possibilities, not options.

# *Abundancy Is Geometrically Dynamic*

The master plan spirit of scarcity is linear and sequential. Scarcity sees the future as being resourced with only those things that are close by. For example, if you start at A and want to get to Z, scarcity sees a long road moving in a linear sequential way through B, C, D, E, and so on. The best resource for the future becomes those steps that are close, or those that seem like they would logically be next. This doesn't leave us with an abundance of options.

On the other hand, the spirit of abundancy sees *every* step as a possible next step. The possibilities are geometrically dynamic. Starting at A again on our way to Z, we see Q as just as viable

> I remember hearing an ancient parable (Babylonian, says Dr. Ethan) about a king and one of his wise subjects who agreed to do a favor for him. The king offered him a fair reward in return for this favor, and his subject asked him for one piece of grain to be placed on one square of a chessboard, two on the second, four on the third, and so on until each square on the chessboard was full. The king laughed at him for his foolishness, thinking that this reward would cost him nothing. But, when the time came to reward his subject for his service, the king found that he did not have enough grain in all his kingdom to fulfill his subject's request. After all, there are 64 squares on a chessboard ($8 \times 8 = 64$), so the king needed to put $2^{63}$ pieces of grain on the final square ($1 = 2^0$ on the first, $1 * 2 = 2^1$ on the second, $1*2*2 = 2^2$ on the third, etc). Considering that $2^{20}$ is about a million (1,048,576 to be exact), $2^{63}$ is more than a million cubed ($2^{63} = 2^{20} * 2^{20} * 2^{20} * 2^3 = (2^{20})^3 * 2^3$), this is a lot of grain. There is some historical debate over whether the king honorably sold his kingdom to pay his debt or whether he beheaded his subject (and whether Babylonians played chess).[3]
>
> —Doctor Andrew, "Squaring Pennies"
> (email reply to junior high math teacher)

a resource for the future as B. Organic order is usually not linear or sequential. The resource possibilities are dimensional and geometric.

The spirit of abundancy is similar to the concept of compound interest. Compound interest is geometrically dynamic. For example, when is $3,769 worth $10,000? Answer: When there is a 5 percent growth rate over twenty years. This growth does not happen in a linear sequential way. Rather, the resources that have been generated now generate more—in a geometrically dynamic way.

So the next time you hold $100, ask yourself, "How much money is this?" Your answer may reflect whether you think in linear sequential ways or in geometrically dynamic ways. If you think you are holding $672.75 (the future value of $100 in twenty years assuming a 10 percent growth rate), you may decide not to spend it.

*A better question for the church might be "What can the church do to assimilate itself into people lives?"*

One way the church has promoted a spirit of scarcity is in its efforts to assimilate people into the master plan of the church. This is a scarcity view of how the church is to be a part of people's lives.

Sometimes we get tunnel vision and think all mission must be accomplished in the church building or in the congregation's name. The church bulletin is full of ministry or study opportunities—all within the walls of the church or its members' homes.

A better question for the church might be "What can the church do to assimilate itself into people lives?" instead of "How can we assimilate people into the church's life?" The church will have a more robust mission in the community (and the world) if it would try to assimilate into people's everyday lives.

One of the things Sara and I appreciate about our congregation is that it values the work we are doing *at work*. Our clients and staff are considered extensions of our church's mission, even though none of them may ever hear the church's name. Any help we might need is freely offered. Nobody at the church is whispering instructions in our ears on how to run our "office ministry." Our workdays are part of the church's story of mission.

As leaders of small groups, what if we asked, "How can we assimilate the church into the groupings people already have in their lives?" It is not the primary purpose of a church to have small groups. Rather, I believe it is a primary responsibility of a church to help people live whole, healthy lives. And as a part of the whole, the church could help people make healthy connections with those they encounter every day.

## Abundancy and Organic Order

As we look back at the chart from chapter 1, which contrasts the master plan approach with the organic order approach, the spirit that emerges from the latter is the spirit of abundancy. As a whole, organic order operates with this spirit of abundancy. And taken individually, each organizational tool has this spirit when used in an organically ordered way. The chart below shows how master plan speaks in a language of scarcity and how organic order speaks in a language of abundance.

| Organizational Tool | Master plan says with a spirit of scarcity: | Organic order says with a spirit of abundance: |
|---|---|---|
| Patterns | Prescriptive<br>*There is a "best" way for people to belong, and this plan will tell them what it is.* | Descriptive<br>*People can belong in a variety of ways, and they are free to belong in one or many ways.* |
| Participation | Representative<br>*People must participate in the way the plan tells them to.* | Individual<br>*People can participate in ways that fit them as individuals.* |
| Measurement | Bottom Line<br>*There is only one way to measure effectiveness.* | Story<br>*Effectiveness can be measured in multiple ways.* |
| Growth | Bankrupt<br>*Resources will only be available at the beginning of a project, and we must maximize their use from the outset.* | Sustainable<br>*Resources will be available through the life of the project, and more resources will become available for the project in the future.* |
| Power | Positional<br>*Power is limited to a few.* | Revolving<br>*Power is shared by several.* |
| Coordination | Cooperation<br>*Control will be built into the plan to avoid disorganization and chaos.* | Collaboration<br>*Everyone's solutions and creativity are invited.* |
| Partners | Accountability<br>*The path to wholeness is a set of laws; our actions are limited to fulfilling those laws.* | Edit-ability<br>*The path to wholeness is grace, which can be shared in a multitude of ways.* |
| Language | Noun-centric<br>*Our experience has limits and can only be expressed in prescribed ways.* | Verb-centric<br>*Words cannot fully express what we are experiencing.* |
| Resources | Scarcity<br>*It is dangerous to presume that we will have enough to meet our needs.* | Abundancy<br>*There will be many opportunities to find resources.* |

The organizational tool of partners has robust possibilities when you see partners through the lens of an author-editor relationship. An accountability relationship that concentrates power in one person's hands limits possibilities. Growth has more opportunity when it is sustainable; growth that leads to bankruptcy limits future potential.

All of the organizational tools will generate a spirit of abundancy when they are used in an organically ordered way. And it is conversely true that when you operate with a spirit of abundancy, you exercise the tools of organic order.

*When you operate with a spirit of abundancy, you exercise the tools of organic order.*

God shares with us his generosity, his grace, and his love with a spirit of abundancy. May we shower in his Spirit, letting the refreshing waters spill onto us and others as we help people with their lives.

# A FINAL WORD
## *organic order*
### moving from programmer to environmentalist

L et's admit it. Trying to develop the next "best practice" is tiring. Coming up with the next big-bigger-biggest program is nerve-racking. Through this book, I've tried to help you shift your thinking from a mindset of programming community to one of using organic order to develop an environment where community can emerge. I'm trying to help you become an environmentalist instead of a programmer.

Environmentalists use the organizational tools in an organic order way. Programmers misuse the organizational tools by using them in a master plan way.

Develop healthy environments where people grow healthy lives. Healthy people grow healthy congregations. Programs do not necessarily grow healthy congregations. One key to creating healthy environments is to avoid making the organic order side of the list into a programming solution. Be relaxed about the organizational tools you use. Keep the organic, well, organic.

It is tempting to think that you have to use all of the organizational tools in an organically ordered way before the environment can become healthy. This is not true. You do not need all of them working well to develop healthy environments. Do not become obsessed with the idea that if you had all of these well in place that you would build the "ultimate" of healthy environments. In nature it is hardly ever true that the environment is ideal or perfect. Rather, when a few elements are well in place, things (and people as well) seem to find their way to healthy growth.

Ken Callahan has taught me much. One idea of his that has helped me most is this: There are many possibilities and you do not need all of them to grow yourself forward in healthy ways. Find the two or three that match your strengths and expand them. Then find another one (maybe two) and grow it forward until it is added as a strength.

Below you will find an exercise to help develop a way forward for you. For each of the tools circle a number from 1 to 10 that best describes the way you primarily use the tool.

|  | Master Plan |  | Organic Order |
|---|---|---|---|
| Patterns | *Prescriptive* | 1 2 3 4 5 6 7 8 9 10 | *Descriptive* |
| Participation | *Representative* | 1 2 3 4 5 6 7 8 9 10 | *Individual* |
| Coordination | *Cooperation* | 1 2 3 4 5 6 7 8 9 10 | *Collaboration* |
| Growth | *Bankruptcy* | 1 2 3 4 5 6 7 8 9 10 | *Sustainability* |
| Measurement | *Bottom Line* | 1 2 3 4 5 6 7 8 9 10 | *Story* |
| Power | *Positional* | 1 2 3 4 5 6 7 8 9 10 | *Revolving* |
| Partners | *Accountability* | 1 2 3 4 5 6 7 8 9 10 | *Edit-ability* |
| Language | *Noun-centric* | 1 2 3 4 5 6 7 8 9 10 | *Verb-centric* |
| Resources | *Scarcity* | 1 2 3 4 5 6 7 8 9 10 | *Abundancy* |

Now circle two or three that are currently in your strength set (a score of 8, 9, or 10) that you think would be fun to expand on. Next underline one or two that you would like to add as a strength. Choose with some wisdom. Choose something that you would enjoy doing, not the one that you think you *should*. Add one that has a score of 5, 6, or 7. It is probably not in your best interest to choose one that has a score of 1, 2, or 3. Be at peace and leave these for a later time.

Now go back and review the corresponding chapters. What are some ideas that came to your mind as you read? What now comes to mind? Develop some simple, relaxed, and fun ways forward.

This exercise will help you begin to shape an environment where people naturally connect—creating art more than manufacturing a product. Our job is to help people with their lives rather than to build infrastructure to help institutions stay alive. Sometimes we focus so much on building a "healthy church" that we forget to tend to the health of people.

Environments are vital—alive. They are not inanimate—dead. When places encourage community to emerge spontaneously, they have motion, emotion, and a living spirit. The goal is not to manufacture community. Neither is the goal to build programs. The hope is to watch living community emerge naturally and collaborate with its environment in helpful, healthy ways.

If there is one place where you can exercise an organic order way, may it be in your own life. Live as an environmentalist for your own life. Create healthy soil for your own growth. This will lead you to understand the environments that will help others.

# A SPECIAL THANKS

I thank those communities that have taught me graceful belonging.

I thank my wife, Sara, who shares her wisdom and love as we grow together. The discoveries shared here have emerged from our relationship. Sara has poured many hours into reworking this book. She is among the best editors in the world. But I thank her mostly for her wise questions and her willingness to listen.

Thanks to Jaclyn, my daughter, for enjoying a spontaneous life, for an unending compassion, and for working hard with hope. I am proud to be your father.

I thank the family at settingPace for the hard work, encouraging words, and friendship. settingPace is a wonderful place to enjoy and experiment with life.

I thank Ken Callahan for his unending wisdom and friendship. Ken's fingerprints are all over this book. He has taught me how to live more robustly and to think more compassionately. Not a word of this work would be possible without him.

Thanks to those friends who have enriched *Organic Com-*

*munity* through their helpful encouragement, wise suggestions, and insightful questions—Jon, Jim, Len, John, Heather, Dwight, Stephanie, Rod and Autumn, Mom, Bill, Brian, Phyllis, Catherine, Randy, Greg, and Doug.

Thanks to the team at Baker who believes in this work. Chad, you are among the best encouraging acquisition editors in the biz. It is a wonderful surprise that this book has brought us together as friends. Paul, you are perceptive and astute. Thanks for making this book better.

Finally, thanks to all who engaged me through reading *The Search to Belong*. Your insights, questions, comments, and encouragement are an invaluable part of developing this material.

# NOTES

### Introduction

1. Peter Block, *The Answer to How Is Yes: Acting on What Matters* (San Francisco: Berrett-Koehler, 2003), ix.

2. Ibid., 38–39.

### Chapter 1  Organic Order

1. Josef Albers, *Interaction of Color*, rev. ed. (New Haven, CT: Yale University Press, 1975), 5.

2. Christopher Alexander and others, *The Oregon Experiment* (New York: Oxford University Press, 1975), 9.

3. Ibid., 23–24.

4. Ibid., 10.

5. Ibid., 18.

6. Ibid., 23.

7. Ibid., 27. The bracketed phrases are my own and are meant to relate this quote about architecture and buildings to community and people. The same is true for the next quote.

8. Ibid., 22–23.

9. Ibid., 25–26.

### Chapter 2  Patterns

1. Kenneth G. Wilson, "Prescriptive and Descriptive Grammar and Usage," *The Columbia Guide to Standard American English* (New York:

Columbia University Press, 1993), 341–42. See online version of this entry at www.bartleby.com/68/45/4745.html.

2. Edward T. Hall, *The Hidden Dimension* (Garden City, NY: Doubleday, 1966; repr., New York: Anchor Books, 1982), 1. Citation is from the Anchor Books edition.

## Chapter 3  Participation

1. David M. Newman, *Sociology: Exploring the Architecture of Everyday Life*, 5th ed. (Thousand Oaks, CA: Pine Forge, 2004). See online version of this book at www.pineforge.com/newman5study/resources/token.htm.

2. Albert Einstein, *The World As I See It*, trans. Alan Harris (1956; repr., New York: Citadel, 2000), 9.

3. David Weinberger, *Small Pieces Loosely Joined: A Unified Theory of the Web* (Cambridge, MA: Perseus, 2002), 115, 120.

4. James Surowiecki, *The Wisdom of Crowds: Why the Many Are Smarter than the Few and How Collective Wisdom Shapes Business, Economies, and Nations* (New York: Doubleday, 2004; repr., New York: Anchor Books, 2005), xix–xx. Citations are from the Anchor Books edition.

5. Bill Fischer and Andy Boynton, "Virtuoso Teams," *Harvard Business Review*, special issue (July/August 2005): 3.

## Chapter 4  Measurement

1. Baseball is now looking at a new way of measuring player performance. See Michael Lewis, *Moneyball: The Art of Winning an Unfair Game* (New York: W. W. Norton, 2003), quoted in Carol Knopes, "Baseball Stats Take on New Meaning as 'Moneyball' Tells Tale," *USA Today*, June 8, 2003, http://www.usatoday.com/money/books/reviews/2003-06-08-moneyball_x.htm (accessed May 29, 2006). According to the dictionary, *sabermetrics* comes from *saber-* (from Society for American Baseball Research) + *-metrics* (as in *econometrics*) and refers to the statistical analysis of baseball data.

2. John Henry quoted in Rob Neyer, "A New Kind of Baseball Owner," *ESPN.com*, August 15, 2002, http://sports.espn.go.com/espn/print?id=1418323&type=columnist (accessed May 29, 2006).

3. Block, *The Answer to How Is Yes*, 78.

4. Jim Collins, *Good to Great and the Social Sectors: A Monograph to Accompany Good to Great* (Boulder, CO: Jim Collins, 2005), 7.

5. Kennon L. Callahan, *Building for Effective Mission: A Complete Guide for Congregations on Bricks and Mortar Issues* (San Francisco: HarperSanFrancisco, 1995), 46.

6. Ibid., 15.

7. Richard A. Jensen, *Thinking in Story: Preaching in a Post-literate Age* (Lima, OH: CSS Publishing, 1993), 18, 19, 21, 24.

## Chapter 5  Growth

1. Alexander and others, *The Oregon Experiment*, 71, 77.

2. Ibid., 67, 76.

3. Collins, *Good to Great and the Social Sectors*, 34.

4. David Jones, "The Case for Patterns in Online Learning," http://cq-pan.cqu.edu.au/david-jones/Publications/Papers_and_Books/webnet99/.

5. William Easterly, *The White Man's Burden: Why the West's Efforts to Aid the Rest Have Done So Much Ill and So Little Good* (New York: Penguin Press, 2006), 30.

## Chapter 6  Power

1. Pat Wingert and Evan Thomas, "On Call in Hell," *Newsweek*, March 20, 2006, 34–43, http://www.msnbc.msn.com/id/11787394/site/newsweek.

2. Al West quoted in Scott Kirsner, "Total Teamwork—SEI Investments," *Fast Company* 14 (April/May 1998): 130, http://www.fastcompany.com/online/14/totalteamwork.html.

3. Rosabeth Moss Kanter, *Executive Excellence*, quoted in Harvey Seifter, "The Conductor-less Orchestra," *Leader to Leader* 21 (Summer 2001): 38–44, http://leadertoleader.org/leaderbooks/l2l/summer2001/seifter.html.

## Chapter 7  Coordination

1. Surowiecki, *The Wisdom of Crowds*, 85–86.

2. Denise VanEck, "The Ache of a Mother" (sermon co-presented with Rob Bell, Mars Hill Bible Church, Grand Rapids, MI, May 5, 2005).

3. Alexander and others, *The Oregon Experiment*, 12.

4. Steven Strogatz, *Sync: The Emerging Science of Spontaneous Order* (New York: Hyperion, 2003), 1.

5. Ibid.

6. Richard Farson, *Management of the Absurd: Paradoxes in Leadership* (New York: Simon & Schuster, 1996), 38, 40–41.

7. Ibid., 39.

8. Ibid., 124.

## Chapter 8  Partners

1. *Merriam-Webster Online Dictionary*, s.v. "accounting," http://www.m-w.com/ (accessed March 20, 2006).

2. "Seven Promises," Promise Keepers, http://www.promisekeepers.org/7Promises.aspx (accessed October 4, 2006) are as follows:

1. A Promise Keeper is committed to honoring Jesus Christ through worship, prayer, and obedience to God's Word in the power of the Holy Spirit.

2. A Promise Keeper is committed to pursuing vital relationships with a few other men, understanding that he needs brothers to help him keep his promises.

3. A Promise Keeper is committed to practicing spiritual, moral, ethical, and sexual purity.

4. A Promise Keeper is committed to building strong marriages and families through love, protection, and biblical values.

5. A Promise Keeper is committed to supporting the mission of his church by honoring and praying for his pastor, and by actively giving his time and resources.

6. A Promise Keeper is committed to reaching beyond any racial and denominational barriers to demonstrate the power of biblical unity.

7. A Promise Keeper is committed to influencing his world, being obedient to the Great Commandment (see Mark 12:30–31), and the Great Commission (see Matthew 28:19–20).

3. "Sample Accountability Questions," Promise Keepers, http://www.promisekeepers.org/FAQ/Men_s%20Ministries,%20Small%20Groups/Sample%20Accountability%20Question.aspx (accessed October 4, 2006).

4. "Christian Accountability—A Need for Support," AllAboutGOD.com, http://www.allaboutgod.com/Christian-Accountability.htm (accessed June 3, 2006).

5. William D. Hendricks, *Exit Interviews* (Chicago: Moody, 1993), 266–67.

6. Floyd K. Baskette, Jack Z. Sissors, and Brian S. Brooks, *The Art of Editing*, 4th ed. (New York: Macmillan, 1986), 5.

7. *The Chicago Manual of Style*, 15th ed. (Chicago: University of Chicago Press, 2003), 73–74.

8. See A.A.'s Twelve Steps, Alcoholics Anonymous, http://www.alcoholics-anonymous.org/en_information_aa.cfm?PageID=17&SubPage=68 (accessed October 31, 2006).

9. Hamilton B. *Twelve Step Sponsorship: How It Works* (Center City, MN: Hazelden, 1996), 75.

### Chapter 9 Language

1. Zdenek Salzmann, *Language, Culture, and Society: An Introduction to Linguistic Anthropology* (Boulder, CO: Westview, 1993), 153, quoted in Stacy Phipps, "Language and Thought: Examining Linguistic Relativity" (paper, December 13, 2001), http://www.ttt.org/linglinks/StacyPhipps.htm (accessed June 4, 2006).

2. Jonathan Alter, "A New Open-Source Politics," *Newsweek*, June 5, 2006, http://www.msnbc.msn.com/id/13006799/site/newsweek (accessed December 4, 2006).

### Chapter 10 Resources

1. Keith Johnstone, *Impro: Improvisation and the Theatre* (London: Eyre Methuen, 1981), 92.

2. Block, *The Answer to How Is Yes*, 4–5.

3. Doctor Andrew, "Squaring Pennies," The Math Forum @ Drexel, http://mathforum.org/library/drmath/view/57918.html (accessed June 11, 2006).

# SELECTED BIBLIOGRAPHY

*Alcoholics Anonymous.* 4th ed. New York: Alcoholics Anonymous World Services, Inc., 2001.

Alexander, Christopher, Murray Silverstein, Shlomo Angel, Sara Ishikawa, and Denny Abrams. *The Oregon Experiment.* New York: Oxford University Press, 1975.

Alexander, Christopher. *The Nature of Order: An Essay on the Art of Building and the Nature of the Universe. Book One: The Phenomenon of Life.* Berkeley, CA: The Center for Environmental Structure, 2002.

————. *The Nature of Order: An Essay on the Art of Building and the Nature of the Universe. Book Two: The Process of Creating Life.* Berkeley, CA: The Center for Environmental Structure, 2002.

————. *The Nature of Order: An Essay on the Art of Building and the Nature of the Universe. Book Three: A Vision of a Living World.* Berkeley, CA: The Center for Environmental Structure, 2002.

————. *The Nature of Order: An Essay on the Art of Building and the Nature of the Universe. Book Four: The Luminous Ground.* Berkeley, CA: The Center for Environmental Structure, 2002.

Al-Khalili, Jim. *Quantum: A Guide for the Perplexed.* London: Weidenfeld & Nicolson, 2003.

Armstrong, David. *Managing by Storying Around: A New Method of Leadership.* New York: Currency, 1992.

Asher, Mark. *Body Language: Easy Ways to Get the Most from Your Relationships, Work and Love Life.* New York: Barnes and Noble Books, 1999.

B. Hamilton. *Twelve Step Sponsorship: How It Works.* Center City, MN: Hazelden, 1996.

Barabási, Albert-László. *Linked: The New Science of Networks.* Cambridge, MA: Perseus Publishing, 2002.

Becker, Howard S. *Outsiders: Studies in the Sociology of Deviance.* New York: The Free Press, 1963, renewed 1991.

Bergquist, William. *The Postmodern Organization: Mastering the Art of Irreversible Change.* San Francisco: Jossey-Bass Publishers, 1993.

Berreby, David. *Us and Them: Understanding Your Tribal Mind.* New York: Little, Brown and Company, 2005.

Biehl, Bobb. *Mentoring: Confidence in Finding a Mentor and Becoming One.* Nashville: Broadman & Holman Publishers, 1996.

Block, Peter. *Stewardship: Choosing Service Over Self-Interest.* San Francisco: Berrett-Koehler Publishers, 1993.

———. *The Answer to How Is Yes: Acting on What Matters.* San Francisco: Berrett-Koehler Publishers, 2003.

Bohl, Charles C. *Place Making: Developing Town Centers, Main Streets, and Urban Villages.* Washington, DC: Urban Land Institute, 2002.

Boyatzis, Richard, and Annie McKee. *Resonant Leadership: Renewing Yourself and Connecting with Others Through Mindfulness, Hope, and Compassion.* Boston: Harvard Business School Press, 2005.

Boynton, Andy, and Bill Fischer. *Virtuoso Teams: Lessons from Teams That Changed Their Worlds.* Harlow, Essex, Great Britain: Pearson Education Limited, 2005.

Buchanan, Mark. *Nexus: Small Worlds and the Groundbreaking Science of Networks.* New York: W. W. Norton, 2002.

Burke, John. *No Perfect People Allowed: Creating a Come as You Are Culture in the Church.* Grand Rapids: Zondervan, 2005.

Christenson, Clayton M., and Michael E. Raynor. *The Innovator's Solution: Creating and Sustaining Successful Growth.* Boston: Harvard Business School Press, 2003.

Clothier, Suzanne. *Bones Would Rain from the Sky: Deepening Our Relationships with Dogs.* New York: Warner Books, 2002.

Cloud, Henry, and John Townsend. *How People Grow: What the Bible Reveals about Personal Growth.* Grand Rapids: Zondervan, 2001.

Cloud, Henry. *Integrity: The Courage to Meet the Demands of Reality: How Six Essential Qualities Determine Your Success in Business.* New York: HarperCollins, 2006.

Denning, Stephen. *The Springboard: How Storytelling Ignites Action in Knowledge-Era Organizations.* Boston: Butterworth Heinemann, 2001.

Donahue, Bill, and the Willow Creek Small Groups Team. *The Willow Creek Guide to Life-Changing Small Groups.* Grand Rapids: Zondervan Publishing House, 1996.

Farson, Richard. *Management of the Absurd: Paradoxes in Leadership.* New York: Simon & Schuster, 1996.

Frey, James. *A Million Little Pieces.* New York: Anchor Books, 2003.

Fugere, Brian, Chelsea Hardaway, and Jon Warshawsky. *Why Business People Speak Like Idiots: A Bullfighter's Guide.* New York: Free Press, 2005.

Gabriel, Yiannis. *Storytelling in Organizations: Facts, Fictions, and Fantasies.* Oxford: Oxford University Press, 2000.

Ginsberg, Scott. *The Power of Approachability: How to Become an Effective, Engaging Communicator One Conversation at a Time.* St. Louis: Front Porch Productions, 2005.

Gladwell, Malcolm. *Blink: The Power of Thinking Without Thinking.* New York: Little, Brown and Company, 2005.

Gorman, Julie A. *Community That Is Christian: A Handbook on Small Groups.* 2nd ed. Grand Rapids: Baker Books, 2002.

Herbold, Robert J. *The Fiefdom Syndrome: The Turf Battles that Undermine Careers and Companies—and How to Overcome Them.* New York: Currency, 2004.

Hesselbein, Frances, Marshall Goldsmith, Richard Beckhard, and Richard F. Schubert, eds. *The Community of the Future.* San Francisco: Jossey-Bass Publishers, 1998.

Holden, Robert. *Success Intelligence: Timeless Wisdom for a Manic Society.* London: Hodder and Stoughton, 2005.

Ingram, Jay. *The Velocity of Honey and More Science of Everyday Life.* Toronto: Penguin Canada, 2003.

Jacobsen, Eric O. *Sidewalks in the Kingdom: New Urbanism and the Christian Faith*. Grand Rapids: Brazos, 2003.

Jacobson, Max, Murray Silverstein, and Barbara Winslow. *Patterns of Home: The Ten Essentials of Enduring Design*. Newtown, CT: The Taunton Press, 2005.

Jaworski, Joseph. *Synchronicity: The Inner Path of Leadership*. San Francisco: Berrett-Koehler Publishers, 1998.

Johnson, Steven. *Emergence: The Connected Lives of Ants, Brains, Cities, and Software*. New York: Scribner, 2001.

Joni, Saj-nicole A. *The Third Opinion: How Successful Leaders Use Outside Insight to Create Superior Results*. New York: Portfolio, 2004.

Kelley, Tom. *The Ten Faces of Innovation: IDEO's Strategies for Beating the Devil's Advocate & Driving Creativity Throughout Your Organization*. New York: Doubleday, 2005.

Kilmann, Ralph H. *Quantum Organizations: A New Paradigm for Achieving Organizational Success and Personal Meaning*. Palo Alto, CA: Davies-Black Publishing, 2001.

Lawrenz, Mel. *Patterns: Ways to Develop a God-Filled Life*. Grand Rapids: Zondervan, 2003.

Leadbeater, Charles. *The Weightless Society: Living in the New Economy Bubble*. New York: Texere, 2000.

Lifton, Walter M. *Working with Groups: Group Process and Individual Growth*, 2nd ed. New York: John Wiley & Sons, 1966.

Lightman, Alan. *A Sense of the Mysterious: Science and the Human Spirit*. New York: Pantheon Books, 2005.

Livio, Mario. *The Golden Ratio: The Story of Phi, The World's Most Astonishing Number*. New York: Broadway Books, 2002.

McGregor, Douglas. *The Human Side of Enterprise*. 25th anniversary printing. New York: McGraw-Hill, 1985.

McKibben, Bill. *Enough: Staying Human in an Engineered Age*. New York: Henry Holt and Company, 2003.

McNeill, William H. *A History of the Human Community, Volume II: 1500 to the Present*. 2nd ed. Englewood Cliffs, NJ: Prentice-Hall, 1987.

Mohn, Reinhard. *An Age of New Possibilities: How Humane Values and an Entrepreneurial Spirit Will Lead Us into the Future*. New York: Crown Publishers, 2004.

Nader, Jonar C. *How to Lose Friends and Infuriate People: Leadership in the Networked World.* Pyrmont, New South Wales, Australia: Plutonium, 2000.

Neuhauser, Peg C. *Corporate Legends and Lore: The Power of Storytelling as a Management Tool.* Austin: PCN Associates, 1993.

Pipher, Mary. *The Middle of Everywhere: Helping Refugees Enter the American Community.* Orlando: Harcourt, 2002.

Plotnik, Arthur. *The Elements of Editing: A Modern Guide for Editors and Journalists.* New York: Collier Books, 1982.

Rheingold, Howard. *Smart Mobs: The Next Social Revolution.* Cambridge, MA: Perseus Publishing, 2002.

Ridley, Matt. *Genome: The Autobiography of a Species in 23 Chapters.* New York: Perennial, 1999.

Sample, Steven B. *The Contrarian's Guide to Leadership.* San Francisco: Jossey-Bass, 2002.

Saul, John Ralston. *The Collapse of Globalism and the Reinvention of the World.* Toronto: Viking Canada, 2005.

Schwartz, Barry. *The Paradox of Choice: Why More Is Less.* New York: HarperCollins, 2004.

Senge, Peter, C. Otto Scharmer, Joseph Jaworski, and Betty Sue Flowers. *Presence: Human Purpose and the Field of the Future.* Cambridge, MA: SoL (The Society for Organizational Learning), 2004.

Simmons, Annette. *The Story Factor: Inspiration, Influence, and Persuasion through the Art of Storytelling.* New York: Basic Books, 2001.

Steinhorn, Leonard. *The Greater Generation: In Defense of the Baby Boom Legacy.* New York: Thomas Dunne Books, 2006.

Stone, Biz. *Blogging: Genius Strategies for Instant Web Content.* Boston: New Riders, 2003.

Stravinsky, Igor. *Poetics of Music in the Form of Six Lessons.* 16th printing. Translated by Arthur Knodel and Ingolf Dahl. Cambridge, MA: Harvard University Press, 1970, 2003.

Strogatz, Steven. *Sync: The Emerging Science of Spontaneous Order.* New York: Hyperion, 2003.

Surowiecki, James. *The Wisdom of Crowds: Why the Many Are Smarter than the Few and How Collective Wisdom Shapes Business, Economies, Societies, and Nations.* New York: Doubleday, 2004.

Taleb, Nassim Nicholas. *Fooled by Randomness: The Hidden Role of*

*Chance in Life and in the Markets.* 2nd ed. New York: Texere, 2004.

Thelen, Herbert A. *Dynamics of Groups at Work: An Application of Social Science to Social Action and Learning, Which Combines Theory with the Insights Born of Classroom and Field Work.* Chicago: University of Chicago Press, 1954.

Watts, Duncan J. *Small Worlds: The Dynamics of Networks between Order and Randomness.* Princeton, NJ: Princeton University Press, 1999.

Weber, Larry. *The Provocateur: How a New Generation of Leaders Are Building Communities, Not Just Companies.* New York: Crown Business, 2001.

Weinberger, David. *Small Pieces Loosely Joined: A Unified Theory of the Web.* Cambridge, MA: Perseus Books Group, 2002.

Wheatley, Margaret J., and Myron Kellner-Rogers. *A Simpler Way.* San Francisco: Berrett-Koehler Publishers, 1999.

Wheatley, Margaret J. *Leadership and the New Science: Discovering Order in a Chaotic World.* 3rd ed. San Francisco: Berrett-Koehler Publishers, 2006.

# INDEX

Joseph R. Myers is an entrepreneur, speaker, and writer. He owns the consulting firm FrontPorch, which helps churches, businesses, and other organizations promote and develop community. Myers is also a founding partner of the communication arts group settingPace, based in Cincinnati, Ohio. He is the author of *The Search to Belong: Rethinking Intimacy, Community, and Small Groups.*

# Also from the ēmersion line . . .

Visit www.emersionbooks.com for the latest ēmersion releases and to find out more about *Organic Community*.

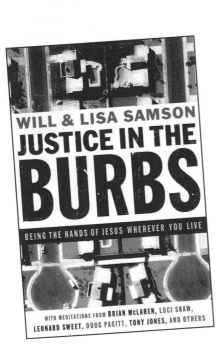

ēmersion: *a partnership between*

**BakerBooks**
*Relevant. Intelligent. Engaging.*
www.bakerbooks.com

emergent
village
www.emergentvillage.com